To: Loren

Phil 4:13

TOTALLY

NAKED AND UNASHAMED

*Exposing the Lies
of the Enemy*

MICHELE TURNER

WESTBOW
P R E S S®
A DIVISION OF THOMAS NELSON
& ZONDERVAN

WestBow Press books may be ordered through booksellers or by contacting:

WestBow Press
A Division of Thomas Nelson & Zondervan
1663 Liberty Drive
Bloomington, IN 47403
www.westbowpress.com
1 (866) 928-1240

Unless marked otherwise, all Scripture quotations are taken from the New King James Version®. Copyright © 1982 by Thomas Nelson. Used by permission. All rights reserved.

Scripture quotations marked KJV are taken from the King James Version.

Scripture quotations marked AMP are taken from the Amplified® Bible, Copyright © 2015 by The Lockman Foundation. Used by permission.

Scripture quotations marked MSG are taken from The Message. Copyright © 1993, 1994, 1995, 1996, 2000, 2001, 2002. Used by permission of NavPress Publishing Group.

ISBN: 978-1-9736-8639-2 (sc)
ISBN: 978-1-9736-8640-8 (hc)
ISBN: 978-1-9736-8638-5 (e)

Library of Congress Control Number: 2020903084

Print information available on the last page.

WestBow Press rev. date: 02/20/2020

CONTENTS

Ken is a fictious character.

INTRODUCTION

No More Games

"Come out, come out, wherever you are!" I played this game when I was a little girl. I would close my eyes and count to ten. The other kids would run and hide while I was counting. Then I would say, "Ready or not, here I come!"

They would hide so well I would sit on my front porch and say, "I am not playing." They hid behind cars and bushes and even inside the house. Today, I am still no longer playing games with anyone, including myself. I am tired of hiding, and I am willing to expose my life for the good of others.

The point of this game was to find those who were hiding. I got tired of looking for people who did not want to be found. Today, it is possible to track people with a cell phone or find their home address by using a GPS. Whether we want to be found or not, we cannot hide. I do not know if you are looking for anyone, but I am looking for Him (God) while He might be found. (See Isaiah 55:6.)

I never thought I would become an author. I have always said no one can tell my story like me. I am my own best spokesperson. I am using this platform as a tool to show the world the transformation of my life. Here I am now, at the point of no return. No need to hide now! God has called me out of darkness.

But you are a chosen generation, a royal priesthood, a holy nation, His own special people, that you may proclaim the praises of Him who called you out of darkness into His marvelous light (1 Peter 2:9).

My exposure to darkness, which I will compare to a photographer's darkroom, was due to my own actions. The late Dr. Myles Munroe said, "When you need fixing, stop going to the devil for parts." I decided to give my heart to Jesus for repair since He has defeated death, hell, and the grave. We have to go inside the darkroom to be fully developed and restored.

The process of developing film begins with the unexposed and undeveloped halide salts. Next, it is converted into a positive image. Finally, the film is fixed, washed, dried, and cut. This is similar to becoming a Christian. First, we have the Father, who handles all who have been exposed to sin. Second, once we accept Jesus the perfect Son, He gives us His image. Third, we have the person of the Holy Spirit, who leads and guides us into all truth with the finishing touches. (See note 1.)

I am not suggesting you have to sin in order to develop. Sin is nothing to play with; it is not a game. However, once you see your picture develop, you realize you have overcome the darkroom. My darkroom is now my prayer room. I go inside for development and to converse with the Godhead (Father, Son, and Holy Spirit). This is how I learned to defeat the devil. I walked in darkness most of my life. I have yielded my life to God for such a time as this, to be a deliverer to His people.

And they overcame him by the blood of the Lamb and by the word of their testimony, and they did not love their lives to the death (Revelation 12:11).

This is my deliverance, with you in mind!

No More Hiding

While seeking the Lord, I asked God why He wanted me to expose myself like this. He whispered in His still small voice (Genesis 2:25), "And they were both naked, the man and his wife, and were not ashamed." This is not a social media post or what people want to hear. My husband, Tim, and I are both unashamed! God has delivered our marriage. To God be all the glory!

Favor is not fair! You may be saying, "How has this chick who came from nothing, with no education, been given the opportunity to write this book?" My response to that question is this: do not allow the events in your life story to define you and put a period at the end of one sentence or moment in your life. Allow God to put His commas, conjunctions, question marks, and periods where He would like. It is not over until God says it is over.

I want to share with you how I was born to Roy and Joyce Thomas. They raised me to the best of their ability. If I may say so, my parents are the best parents a girl could ask for. My parents loved me unconditionally. Even though they saw me at my worst and rarely at my best, they never judged me. They always told me that I had a good husband. My mom loved her father, John Henry Lee, and she always said he was the greatest man she ever knew—until she met her son-in-law (whom she referred to as son), Timothy Turner Sr.

The first time Tim and I shared our testimony, we were asked to speak at a Bride of Christ life event. I went to the event convinced that I would only tell them what I wanted them to know. I did not want to share completely because I felt I was in a room filled with women who did not like me and would judge me by my past. Right before it was our turn to speak, my nose began to bleed. I went to the restroom, and looking at myself in the mirror, I could clearly hear God saying, "I am going to strip you naked with nothing left to hide. This is for My glory and your good." From that moment forward, I knew that no one would ever be able to hold anything over my head about my past—not even me.

Exposing the Lies

At the beginning of each chapter, I will share with you the lies the enemy whispered to me because I allowed him to be too close to me. I have now learned that he is defeated and stripped of all influence over me. I now command him to back up and come no closer because he is trespassing. He is not wanted. I am God's property. I will strip those lies from your mind by using the Word of God to reveal His truth.

I would like to define the way God viewed nakedness and my own personal view before I became saved:

God:

Never intended for Adam to Kaput the covenant between himself and God by blaming Eve. The Decree was made between God and Adam, not Eve. Again, God Never made His covenant with Eve. So Adam disobeyed God by eating the fruit; we are all now born into Sin.

Me:

Never tell me no. Anyway, it is my way or the highway. I always Keep it real. I Enticed others to do wrong. Do not get in my way. I am a girl on the move. I Needed no one's approval. I am Enough for anybody and everybody. A Smooth operator. I was a Sinner.

ACKNOWLEDGMENTS

Thanks be to God Almighty for the journey He has taken me on. It is a journey that has resulted in me becoming who I am today. I love my family—my husband, Timothy W. Turner Sr., my children, Quanika, Tim Jr., and Faith. My family has been there through my ups and downs, the good and bad. I truly love them from the heart—*fam4love*. I could not have accomplished writing this book without the love and encouragement of my family. They inspire me to be the best that I can be!

I pen this book with the help of the person of the Holy Spirit. I do not have a GED or high school diploma, but Colossians 2:6–8 says, "As you therefore have received Christ Jesus the Lord, so walk in Him, rooted and built up in Him and established in the faith, as you have been taught, abounding in it with thanksgiving. Beware lest anyone cheat you through philosophy and empty deceit, according to the tradition of men, according to the basic principles of the world, and not according to Christ."

Many men and women of God have helped me spiritually to grow into the woman of God that I am today. Many thanks to the men and women of God who have impacted my life over the past twenty years. A special thank you to my bishop and pastor, Derek and Yeromitou Grier (Grace Church, Virginia), for allowing me to minister to God's people alongside you.

A heartfelt thank you to my sisters in Christ, Pam King and Audrey Ellis, for believing in my story in its birthing stage.

Exposing the Lies
You were a mistake.

1. Why were you born? Why are you here? The world would have been a much better place without you.

Before I formed you in the womb I knew you;
Before you were born I sanctified you;
I ordained you a prophet to the nations.
—Jeremiah 1:5

CHAPTER 1

I Am Willing to Expose Me to Help You

When I talk about exposure, I want you to think of an x-ray test. Typically, you get an x-ray because the doctor needs to view the inside of your body without having to make an incision. I pray this book allows you to see inside of yourself through my life without the cuts, stitches, and bruises. A voice must cry out in the wilderness, just like John the Baptist, preparing the way. I want my voice to prepare the way for our soon-coming King.

The Holy Spirit desires to live inside of His children, but many are illegitimate because His love has been rejected. The Lord sees all the wickedness on the earth as if He is looking at an x-ray. For so long, I gave Christianity a bad name, and I now understand why God said He regretted ever creating humankind (Genesis 6:6). I wanted to change God's mind about me, so I repented of my many sins.

As a result, I have not seen the destruction I deserved. I have found favor with God, just as Noah and his family did during the storm of great destruction. When God wanted to bring structure back into the earth, He used a body in the person of His son Jesus Christ. So I say, expose me, Lord, to speak back to the world.

I know that just as God spoke to Jeremiah the prophet, the same is true for me. I am here today to allow the manifestation of who God ordained me to be for His glory. This is my declaration: "The Spirit of the Lord *is* upon Me, Because He has anointed Me To preach the gospel to *the* poor; He has sent Me to heal the brokenhearted, To proclaim liberty to *the* captives And recovery of sight to *the* blind, *To* set at liberty those who are oppressed; To proclaim the acceptable year of the Lord" (Luke 4:18–19; italics added). As you read this book, you will see the power of God at work in a life submitted to the will of God.

The Baby Girl Is Born

I was born to Roy and Joyce Thomas, natives of Washington, DC, on August 3, 1968. My dad wanted to name me after his mother, Alberta, and my mom would not have it! Since they could not agree, I was named Michele Thomas. As a result of their disagreement, in 2002 when I needed a copy of my birth certificate, I discovered that it did not have a name on it. How funny is that? I am the baby girl out of five birth siblings plus one.

My mom referred to us as the "Jive Five Plus One." Growing up, there was a rival distinguishing our blended families as the Thomases and the Fergusones (my older siblings have a different dad). We could tease each other, but no one from the outside could do it, or there would be a fight!

Growing Up in My House

I remember all the girls slept in one room, and the boys in another room. I was always afraid of the dark. At night, I would cry for someone to go with me to the bathroom. I would pee in the bed if no one went with me. This eventually stopped as I got older. My siblings would tease me because of this, but I did not care.

I did not have much hair when I was little, and my siblings used to call me "Bald Dina." I created long hair by putting towels on my head and pretending it was my own. My mom would spank my siblings if they touched or made fun of my fake towel hair. (Getting my way began very early, contributing to selfishness and thinking life was all about me.)

I love wearing different hairstyles. I wear all colors of wigs, quick weaves, and braids. I am confident with my wigs, and I am not pretending it is my real hair. I will wear a white wig on Sunday and a red wig on Wednesday. I embrace my creativity. Thank God for wigs because I love the variety of styles available.

My Parents' Love

I was spoiled because I was my daddy's baby girl. I could get away with just about anything if I cried to my daddy. However, this benefit did not last very long because, for most of my childhood, my dad was in prison. Even though he was not there, I knew he loved me, and I definitely loved him. I always looked forward to our visits at the Lorton Correction Center.

When my mom would take us to the prison, I would tell on her if she had other men in the house. I was the one who sat on my dad's lap and got all the hugs and kisses. The love my dad demonstrated to me during those visits was profound. His love kept the bars and prison doors from interfering with the love I had for him.

As a daddy's girl, I believed that the universe revolved around me. I learned very quickly that I would be easily defended, and my looks brought attention to me. My biological father is no longer here, but I treasure the time spent with him. He was not always around, but the time I spent with him is forever mine.

On one occasion, my dad stayed over at my house, and at three o'clock in the morning, he was up cleaning. It is no wonder I think the house has to always be spic and span. Roy Thomas will forever be in my heart, and I thank him for the memories.

It would take an entire book to write about Joyce Thomas, the best mother in the world. This lady would take care of her Jive Five Plus One and any of our friends that we brought home. She was a giver of love. She always thought of others before herself. I describe her this way, "She *is* more precious than rubies, And all the things you may desire cannot compare with her" (Proverbs 3:15; italics added).

My mom lived to be seventy-five years old. My family and I served as her caregivers. We would not have had it any other way because she held a special place in our hearts. The Bible instructs us to take care of our parents and honor them (see Exodus 20:12). I honor her for loving me always. She is my "Joycie Baby" forever.

My mom shared a powerful word with me years ago. She said, "Marriage is the hardest job in the world because you never get a day off or a vacation." She went on to say, "You cannot quit because God hates divorce!" Even though she divorced twice, I learned from her wisdom that if I am willing to put in the hours and work overtime, I will reap the best benefits.

You have to work hard at your marriage if you want it to last. I was lazy concerning my marriage. I did not invest in it. I should have given more to my marriage—more communication, quality time, and long-term investments. I am still learning to put time and perks into my marriage in order to reap the benefits of a good, godly marriage.

My mom loved my dad so much that no matter where he was or what he did, she always took him back. She even went inside of crack houses to get him. Every time he went to prison, she was there for him. My dad's family always gave love and honor to my mom for taking such good care of my dad.

God Created You with Purpose

I will not blame my upbringing for the choices I made in life, whether it be fornication, adultery, or any sin I have committed. I made bad choices freely with only one thing in mind—me! I had myself on my mind all of the time. I wanted what I wanted when and how I wanted it.

How do you get to the place where you do not know who you are or why you are there? It begins with an incomplete understanding of why you were created. Understanding our purpose is a necessary process in order to move beyond reckless behaviors. First of all, it is vital that we realize and experience the love of God. Second, we must not place our value in the absence or presence of love in our childhood.

Too many excuses contribute to seeking validation from the wrong sources because of the lack of self-love. Many of us struggle today because we do not know who we are, so we try to fit in with the crowd. I struggled with this because I fed the wrong image of my identity. We need to follow the person of the Holy Spirit in order to find our identity. I am not defined by the color of my skin, the house I live in, or my bank accounts. I am a child of the Most High God. I am still a daddy's girl. Thank You, Abba Father.

God's love is immeasurable, and He Sent His only Son for each of us to have eternal life (John 3:16).

Do you love yourself? The root of not understanding your purpose can also be detected by the blame game. Loving yourself takes away the excuses of the actions of others. It is essential to believe that God loves you and that He had a purpose in mind for you from the very beginning. A lack of self-love left me falling in love with the things of a fallen world.

The earth spins at an incredible speed. The force of gravity holds each of us from flying out into outer space. Where will you land on that day when it all stops? When you start loving yourself, you will stop negotiating with your life. It is not a debate. I am no longer transferring ownership of my life to others or my foolish ways.

I have learned to appreciate the stop sign. When you come to a complete stop, you can look both ways and take a pause, even if it is for one second. Love allows you to stop, reflect, and take a breath as you think of His unfailing love. Learn to never settle for anything less than God's best for you. Unfortunately, I settled. It was a journey. Read on!

Sin Produces Death

Don't love the world's ways. Don't love the world's goods. Love of the world squeezes out love for the Father. Practically everything that goes on in the world—wanting your own way, wanting everything for yourself, wanting to appear important—has nothing to do with the Father. It just isolates you from Him. The world and all its wanting, wanting, wanting is on the way out—but whoever does what God wants is set for eternity (1 John 2:15–17, The Message Bible).

Lust of the Flesh

Our flesh is muscle and fat found between skin and bones. The skin is a thin layer of tissue forming the natural outer covering of the body. Donor sites are made to move skin from a noninjured area of the body to cover a burn or wound. The skin will attach itself and help heal the wound. It takes about fourteen days to heal. During the healing process, you must keep the site moist to avoid dryness and itching.

Our flesh is not meant to be uncovered. That is why skin is grafted (donor site) in order to prevent exposure. The dermatologist recommends that the skin be kept dry due to small gaps forming in the skin barrier. The possibility of bacteria and fungus is increased with any open areas in the skin. (See note 2.)

The clothing industry earns billions designing clothes that keep us covered, whether it's Walmart, Neiman Marcus, Target, or Bloomingdales. Some of the items, such as ripped jeans or jeans with holes in them, show extra skin, but the body is still covered. A more conservative person would say that jeans with holes are not appropriate for certain venues. In fact, a fully clothed person could be judged as being half-naked simply because of the style of clothing. What happens when you do not have your body covered properly?

In Genesis 9:22, we read, "And Ham, the father of Canaan, saw the nakedness of his father, and told his two brothers outside." The word *nakedness* in Hebrew means disgrace or shame. There are times when I have been a disgrace to my family and brought shame on us because of my nakedness. Noah got drunk off of the wine, and his son used this opportunity to expose instead of cover his nakedness. Thank God for Shem and Japheth, as they walked backward to cover their father's nakedness.

God never intended for our nakedness to be shameful. I did not honor God with my body; therefore, it did not matter what label I had on. My thoughts when I put on my clothes, whether covered up or not, were not to represent God. I was thinking, *Girl, I am cute.*

Eve was trying to be cute too (see Genesis 3:6). She had three things on her mind; it was good, pleasant, and would make her wise. When I was in the world, these were the same qualities I looked for. I never considered the cost. Oh, what a price there is to pay.

After Adam ate the fruit, they knew they were naked. Adam and Eve tried to hide their nakedness from God. God clothed them because He is a loving God (see Genesis 3:8, 21). I must admit that I was not being smart while trying to live out there in those streets. I was heading for an early death or jail. I had to learn to stop hiding and making dumb decisions.

Jesus came to redeem our bodies back. Paul taught the Church at Corinth, "Now the body *is* not for sexual immorality but for the Lord, and the Lord for the body" (1 Corinthians 6:13). Our spirit man is more important than the body. Jesus is your surefire protection from hell when you have accepted Him as Lord and Savior.

If your flesh is dictating your every move, you may not die today, but spiritually you are separated from God. Stop caring more about your flesh than your soul. Paul tells us that if anyone had a right to be confident in the flesh, it was him (see Philippians 3:4–6). As a woman, I am drawn emotionally—how I felt became my priority.

The lust of the flesh asks, "Does it feel good? Does it feel cozy? Does it rock me to sleep at night? In the middle of the night, am I lying in the wrong bed asking myself why am I here?" It's self-validation from making the wrong man feel good. Sex never defined my purpose. I defined my purpose by having sex. Due to my self-seeking will, my desires were not His desires.

Lust of the Eyes

The eye lenses focus the light rays that pass through (and into the retinae) in order to create clear images. During an eye exam, they ask you to look straight ahead without blinking. You are then instructed to follow the point of a pin while they check to see if your eye lenses are focused.

Satan convinced me for so long to focus on my sinful life. In spite of all that I had going on, God protected me from me. My saying was, "If I like it, I am going to have it!" Nothing was going to stop me because I had my eyes fixed on what I wanted. I knew that I was unstoppable, but the problem was I was a danger to myself and others. I was a time bomb waiting to explode. I have always been confident, with a fierce "I cannot lose" attitude, but in the past, I was also very cold.

What do you see? *What do you see?* <u>What do you see?</u> *What do you see?*

Be careful to keep your eyes on Jesus.

Looking unto Jesus, the author and finisher of *our* faith, who for the joy that was set before Him endured the cross, despising the shame, and has sat down at the right hand of the throne of God (Hebrews 12:2).

God blinded Paul so that he could see that his zeal was in persecuting the church and he was abiding under the law. I was blinded, seeing only what I wanted to see. My eyes were deceived most of the time. I had to get my eyes examined in order for my vision to align with His.

Do not get stuck with tunnel vision like I did. This type of vision causes you to focus on a single point of view. God is all-seeing; that is why we call Him El Roi. Instead of seeking God to ask Him, "Is this the man you want for me?" I learned to settle, because what God wanted for me may have taken too much time. Use time wisely. It is something you can never get back.

On the subway, you are sure to catch a glance of the man and woman sitting so close that you cannot separate them. This couple looks happy. They appear to have it all together in love. What we do not understand from what we see is their truth. Are they a couple that just joined together for sexual fulfillment? Are they two people who settled for doing things the world's way? It is easier to settle and be with the wrong person than to be alone. In reality, we are never alone (see Deuteronomy 31:6).

I enjoyed sin. I enjoyed what I was doing. The world glamorizes sin. It makes sin look pretty, fun, and exciting. Sin is a choice (see Hebrew 11:25). The enemy had nothing on me. My thoughts, my mind, my will, my emotions—I was Michele doing Michele at the highest level.

We have to endure, be patient, and fight for what God wants for us. The enemy tells us to go ahead in sin, convincing us that it is not so bad. Sin looks and sounds good, but at the root of it, if you really look with the lenses of your eyes, it produces death (see Romans 6:23).

Pride

Pride is arrogance of demeanor, self-trust, and the opposite of humility. Since we have all free will, Salt & Pepa (female rap group, 1988) said it best, "It's your thing, do what you want to do." For so long, I really believed I could do what I wanted to do.

I watched the movie *Pride*, a 1970 film about a Philadelphia swim team. The coach, with the help of a janitor, fixed up an abandoned building for the team. They had to fight racism, violence, and a hostile city official to compete with an all-black swim team. From this movie, I learned you must overcome pride and failure and defeat racism. Pride promotes strife.

Had I become a racist toward God? Did I feel superior in my flesh, above His ways? I was a black woman who trusted no one, not even God. I had to allow God to fix me up. I was just like an abandoned building—cold and empty. I trusted my flesh more than my spirit. There was a battle going on.

During this season in my life, the Geto Boys, a hip-hop group from the nineties, spoke my truth when they said, "My mind was playing tricks on me." Now I cast down every thought that tries to fight against my spirit.

Pride is knowing what I should do but not wanting to do it. Thoughts ran through my mind, such as, *I feel validated by making this man feel good. I do not want anyone to know that I struggle with pride. If I do not have sex with him, will he leave me?* The enemy plants strategic thoughts to trap you in pride.

Pride is like a bacteria; you cannot see it, but it infects. As an adulteress, I was like a bacteria in many homes. Inside the body, bacteria can cause pain. I have already mentioned how I love everything to be clean. As an example, raw chicken left on the countertop causes the spread of bacteria. If you try to wipe it up without disinfectant, the bacteria remains on the sponge. I would come into men's lives and eat away at their home. I would make them leave their wives.

The bacteria was also eating away at me and everyone around me. I had to go back to the roots of what I knew. God had to show me myself. He told me that I had to die to myself.

Tim was the disinfectant that would assist in cleaning me up. However, I did not know how to appreciate him. I also used the power of influence or manipulation on him. I knew what to say and how to say it. I would speak soothing words to Tim to get what I wanted. Because the bacteria was so strong, Tim could not tell me no! I was using my ability to influence him so that I could do me.

How do you kill pride within you? James teaches us, "Therefore submit to God. Resist the devil and he will flee from you. Draw near to God and He will draw near to you. Cleanse *your* hands, *you* sinners; and purify *your* hearts, you double-minded" (James 4:7–8). We need to call sin what it is!

I understood that my ways could end someone up in hell. When I was in sin and heard of my girlfriends who were also fornicating or committing adultery, I encouraged them, and we would laugh about it. In my pride, I gave ungodly counsel. If she had a "boo" or a boyfriend, I would ask her if he had a friend for me. This is what happens when we do not know who we are. We compromise. Do not let pride stop you from getting godly counsel (see Psalm 1:1).

Selfishness

I was being selfish. I was just being Michele! I did not see selfishness as God defines it. I believed it was my world! Occasionally, when I was younger, all of us kids would get in trouble and have to get a spanking. I would always go last, and then I would say to my dad, "Daddy, I don't want a beating!" Quickly I learned that this worked for me and decided that I should always be last in the lineup.

I did not think that this was selfishness. I thought I was being smart. We have to learn that there are consequences for our actions. You should not expect to always get away with everything.

My dad always told me I was smart, beautiful, and gorgeous. I grew up thinking that my looks and my body would get me whatever I wanted. For the most part, it worked. I would walk down the street, and someone would yell, "Hey, shawty!" I would think to myself, *I got him locked and loaded.*

When I married Tim, he was exactly the way he is today. He tried to please me whether he agreed or not. He thought I would change my behavior if he gave me what I wanted. He did not realize when he met me that was not what I needed. He did not know how deeply selfishness was rooted within me.

He showed me his hand of cards. My attitude was, "If you cannot make this happen, I will find someone who can." Tim did anything and everything I wanted, but still it was never enough. You cannot satisfy a selfish person. Selfish people are self-seeking and self-serving and have self-interest only in themselves.

I love playing a card game of spades. When I have a good hand, I talk big trash. Why? Because I know I am "Boss Lady!" This is especially true when I know that the other person has nothing in his hand. My attitude rises to another level of confidence with arrogance in my voice. Thankfully, God showed us His hand! We win. Game over!

The Snatcher

To snatch means to grab, seize, lay (one's) hands on.

I know what being snatched physically feels and looks like. Growing up, I got snatched all the time. I got snatched by my shirt and sent down the stairs by myself into the dark.

I have also snatched my children. If they were smart-mouthed, I would grab them by their shirts, letting them know I am the momma. Our loving God has snatched the covers off of me so that I can willingly expose myself for His glory.

The bad decisions we make will eventually cause us to be exposed, just as Adam and Eve were exposed. When God created humankind, He never intended for us to be ashamed about anything.

And they were both naked, the man and his wife, and were not ashamed (Genesis 2:25).

He created us on purpose to be like Him spiritually. We were not created to be equal with God but after His own image. We are not perfect beings, and we have always had free will to choose. I misused my free will; it was not submitted to the Father. I have been trying to hide for too long.

They tried to hide from God. Imagine that! I refuse to be like Adam and Eve any longer, trying to sew fig leaves together to cover up my sin (see Genesis 3:7). God has called my name, and I say, "Here I am, Lord. Use me!"

Move Quickly

Many of us are like the turtle moving slowly to obey God, but I pray that you will not wait until it is too late. We can all relate to the turtle. The turtle's shell is made from its rib cage, and its spine is attached to the internal bones. Eve was also created from a rib. The turtle's shell is hard in order to provide protection. (See note 3.)

Our behavior can become like the shell, causing us to believe that we are untouchable. Adam was Eve's protector, but he did not say anything about Eve eating that fruit right in front of him. They were removed from the garden, and sin has plagued the human race because of Adam's disobedience.

Without godly guidance, we act just like the turtle. We stand in the road, assuming we will never get hit. Let me tell you, you are not untouchable! You must learn to deal with the real you ... without the mask. You might live long, but you just might end up in hell. I escaped hell, so allow me to share my story with you.

A Relationship with God

If we do not know who we are in Christ, we will never be able to break free. Considering my past, I realized that every day I looked at myself in the mirror, I had to choose Christ instead of Michele. I had to choose Him each day. I had to choose to serve God and not Michele. I had to choose that today will be a better day in Christ, instead of without Christ.

I would say a prayer to God, but I did not know Him as Abba Father. As a little girl, I knew how much my dad loved me. With the understanding of my dad's love and then learning that God was called Abba Father, I realized I wanted the relationship to work because of the instability in my history of relationships. I wanted to give God a try. I knew of Him, but I did not yet trust Him. I was not sure if the relationship was going to work out.

In the beginning of our relationship, I dealt with the tough questions. Am I going to use God like I used every other man? Would I allow Him to use me according to the plans He had for me? I would awake in the morning and ask God, "What do You want me to do?" I spoke to Him just as I would speak to my earthly father. We keep it real!

I found God to be true, without an error in His record. I yielded to Him. God was the first man I encountered to be faithful and trustworthy. I fell in love with God, who I've never seen physically, but His touches are so intimate. I never felt violated from His touch. He allowed me to cry and laugh all at the same time, without being judgmental.

On several occasions, I heard people say, "Check His track record!" From that, I learned that not only would He not fail me, He could not fail me! I had experienced a new love, and my understanding of relationships changed. I could be faithful to my husband and children but most of all to myself. Today I have found a safeguard in seeking God and doing things His way. The power is being obedient to the Word of God that tells us who we are.

The Naked Truth
*****

Open your heart to see the real you. Deal with the root of your problem and not just the fruit.

Michele's Heart
*****

Thank You, God, that You desire to deliver women, men, young girls, and young boys from the spirit of adultery and fornication. In our mother's womb, You already had a purpose for us. We came into a world full of sin, and instead of trusting in You, we allowed television to deform and reshape our minds and thoughts. We will not allow the internet, Hollywood, family, or friends to define us, but we will search out Your Word. We were created with purpose, power, and destiny. Nothing fulfills us until we do what You have called us to do. We were created to rule and have dominion. We have dominion over our bodies, and no longer will we sin against our bodies. We yield the fruit of our bodies, and we give it over to You.

Exposing the Lies
Shush! No one will ever know!

2. What would people say if they knew your entire story?

> For there is nothing covered that will not be
> revealed, nor hidden that will not be known.
> —Luke 12:2

CHAPTER 2

Who Told You That You Were Naked?

When I think of nakedness, I see a person without clothes. The magazines *Playboy* and *Vogue* have made nakedness look good, to the point of women wearing *anything* to work and to church. It is as if they are modeling for the *Vogue* nude section. Nothing is left for the imagination, considering what is underneath the clothes.

God asked Adam and Eve who told them that they were naked. He did not ask this because He did not know; He wanted them to tell Him what they had done. Then He asked the main question, "Have you eaten from the tree of which I commanded you that you should not eat?" (Genesis 3:11). We find Adam and Eve wanting to be covered because they were ashamed of their nakedness. They knew the difference between decency and indecency. Seeing my nakedness as a bad thing, I recall being able to relate to their experience.

Have you ever lied to God? Unfortunately, I have lied millions of times and found myself so far away from Him that I did not really believe in Him, His promises, or that He could save someone like me because I was so naked. I truly have felt like Judas once or twice in my life. I betrayed God, lied on Him, and if I could have sold Him, I would have. I was in need of God because He was the only one who could save me and deliver me from me.

I know God never intended for me to live my life with such a seducing attitude, but I did. I never operated in witchcraft, but that is what the seducing spirit attempts to do to you. It will trap you and deceive you, taking your innocence. Like it or not, Satan was my daddy because I allowed him to let my nakedness become my blemish. Why could I not see God? John has this answer as we read, "The Spirit of truth, whom the world cannot receive, because it neither sees Him nor knows Him" (John 14:17).

I was nude with no outer garments because I chose not to cover myself with God's righteousness. I chose to live a life of sin. I will call that sin what it was ... fornication. Do not get caught in the trap of the world system that is passing away. Please be concerned with Him who can kill the soul and the body (see Matthew 10:28).

Jesus was crucified on the cross naked because of the sins of the world (see 1 John 2:2). I would like to inform you that His death was not in vain. His nakedness was with a purpose. We will pay the penalty of our sins if we do not repent. We must have a change of mind and behavior.

We need people in our lives to tell us when we are naked. Nakedness is more than not wearing clothes. I researched women getting strip-searched in prison. This is known as the common strip-search routine and takes nakedness to another level. The female inmates are given the following commands: take your hair down, lift your breasts and stomach (if necessary), squat and cough, cough harder, squat lower, turn around, shake your head, bend over and spread your butt cheeks, spread them wider, and get dressed. The strip search process is necessary for all women due to contraband and theft. (See note 4.)

I know that may be a bit much for those who are holier than thou, but I know what it is to have been a sinner and now a saint. When God strip-searched me, He knew I had to go through this process because I was still carrying some stuff with me. He knew the old Michele would try to hide stuff and still sneak it into the church. My lies and tricks would have come right to the front row with me. Understand that you can bring it to church, but you cannot get into heaven with it.

Do you not know that the unrighteous will not inherit the kingdom of God? Do not be deceived. Neither fornicators, nor idolaters, nor adulterers, nor homosexuals, nor sodomites, nor thieves, nor covetous, nor drunkards, nor revilers, nor extortioners will inherit the kingdom of God (1 Corinthians 6:9–10).

Adam and Eve knew they were naked due to their disobedience to God. That is why they hid. Many of us go through the common strip search process because we have broken the justice system of God's law. Truthfully, I tell you I felt like I was walking in downtown DC without clothes at times. I was the talk of the town in many of my family and friends' conversations. My nakedness was exposed, and no one took the time to tell me, "I see you, and go put on some clothes!" I had on clothes but was still nude spiritually. I was just like Adam and Eve due to my disobedience.

The Root of My Nakedness

Please understand that God never intended for us to have sex before marriage. What led me to sexual perversion and fornication in my adolescence? As a child, I knew that there was something different about me because my nakedness was dysfunctional. I began to hide by assuring myself that my behavior was natural. As an adult, I started seeking Him, and God revealed to me that this nakedness started years ago.

I believe that God has shielded me from the traumatic experience. Someone or something awakened sexual behaviors inside of me that I attempted to satisfy. I am not only writing about what the Bible says but from experience.

> And since they did not see fit to acknowledge God
> *or* consider Him worth knowing [as their Creator],
> God gave them over to a depraved mind, to do
> things which were improper *and* repulsive, until
> they were filled (permeated, saturated) with every
> kind of unrighteousness, wickedness, greed, evil;
> full of envy, murder, strife, deceit, malice *and* mean-
> spiritedness. They are gossips [spreading rumors],
> slanders, haters of God, insolent, arrogant, boastful,
> inventors [of new forms] of evil, disobedient *and*
> disrespectful to parents, without understanding,
> untrustworthy, unloving, unmerciful [without pity].
> (Romans 1:28–31 Amplified)

The struggle was real for a long time. That is why I am telling my truth, to help someone else or make others aware of how we need to watch our children.

Be very careful who you allow to watch your children. A person that looks normal may be very dysfunctional on the inside. Remember, there is a root behind everything that happens to and within us. We have an adversary and he is always on his job. "The thief does not come except to steal, and to kill, and to destroy" (John 10:10). One wrong touch can leave you in a lifetime of bondage.

The Touch of Bondage

Touch is one of our five senses. Touch is responsible for all sensation we feel—hot, cold, rough, smooth, pressure, vibration, and much more. Your hand is a touch receptor. Our ability to perceive touch sensations gives our brain a wealth of information about our environment, such as temperature, pain, and pressure. It is considered rapidly adapting if it responds to a change of stimulus very quickly. (See note 5.)

For example, when you touch a hot object, you remove your hand very quickly because it knows when it touched the hot object and when it was removed from the hot object. The problem with the rapidly adapting receptor is you. It cannot tell you how long the skin touched the object. You can get burned before you know it. The main focus is the wrong touch, hot or cold, will leave you in bondage/burned.

Bondage is slavery. I know personally that whether you want to be or not, you are captured by this touch until God gives you freedom. I have cried out many times, "For we know that the law is spiritual, but I am carnal, sold under sin" (Romans 7:14). I was a slave to sin.

I am reminded of Tamar, the daughter of King David, after her brother, Amnon, raped her. "So she said to him, "No, indeed! This evil of sending me away is worse than the other that you did to me." But he would not listen to her. Then he called his servant who attended him and said, "Here! Put this woman out, away from me, and bolt the door behind her" (2 Samuel 13:16–17).

Whoever touched me sent me away like Amnon sent Tamar, without letting anyone know. That person bolted the door on the secret that became a stronghold for me. I would not be rid of this sexual bondage until years later when I was married with children. God had to show me that it was not of Him and that it was a demonic spirit that I was allowing to control me.

The Immoral Woman

> For the lips of an immoral woman drip honey, and
> her mouth is smoother than oil; but in the end she
> is bitter as wormwood, sharp as a two-edged sword.
> Her feet go down to death, her steps lay hold of hell.
> Lest you ponder her path of life—Her ways are
> unstable; you do not know them. (Proverbs 5:3–6)

I caution the men to be aware of smooth-talking women because we are a force to be reckoned with. We know all the words to say to get in your head. We know how to charm you. Oh my, please do not kiss us! Remember Judas betrayed Jesus with a kiss (see Luke 22:48). Judas's kiss marked Jesus as being the one who the soldiers would arrest and later kill.

Judas was one of the twelve disciples. He was in Jesus's inner circle. A kiss on the cheek, in that culture, was a sign of respect, honor, and brotherly love. Judas used his kiss as a sign to turn on Jesus, who is love.

Typically, when you let someone kiss you, they are close to you. When we are in a relationship, we do not normally kiss on the cheek like Judas, but the broken trust is still the same.

Faithful are the wounds of a friend, but the kisses of an enemy are deceitful (Proverbs 27:6).

An immoral woman will leave you with a mark of death. In today's society, couples break up, and it is not uncommon that one of them plans to have the other murdered or to murder them by their own hands. I know you do not want to hear this, but one touch can cause entrapment because of the lonely feeling you are left with.

The wrong image will leave an imprint on your mind that will cause you to become depressed. Have you ever seen something, walked away, and that image stayed on your mind all day? That is how I felt as an immoral woman. I thought about me all day. This is how stroking an obsession happens, because you ponder that thing way too long. If you are not serious, keep your hands and mouths off of people.

I never needed for a man to validate me. Remember, I always thought I was a grape soda and a bag of chips! The fornication spirit attached itself to me because I allowed the lustful spirit to remain too long. At this point, I had a choice to make, and I chose to sow to my flesh instead of my spirit (see 1 Corinthians 6:18). You may be thinking, *Wow, how could this be?*" Please understand when we do not acknowledge Him, we really are rejecting Him.

Paul informs the Romans that God allowed them to become lovers of themselves due to their disobedience (see Romans 1:24). I battled the lustful spirit until I became a true disciple of Jesus Christ.

The problem with most of us is we have not learned how to overcome. You think no one can see you. Baby, you see you and you know! You have locked those secrets in the cave right along with *you*. You lie to yourself every day, saying, "It is okay. I will be alright as long as no one else finds out." Let me tell you, you are not okay, and thinking like that, you will never be okay. You do not have to be like me and share your story with the world, but please tell someone.

And they overcame him by the blood of the Lamb and by the word of their testimony (Revelation 12:11).

Stripped out of Bondage

Many of us have seen a stripper, whether at a party, on television, or in a club. As a male or female, we may have thrown money at them, had a lap dance, or something. God wanted to strip me free of me; that was my bondage. He took me back to the root of the problem. I said to God, "If You are real, show Yourself to me." When I wanted to go back to my behavior, He would remind me of my image in the mirror—the naked, stripped Michele. The Holy Spirit had shown me that my actions were demonic.

A root is defined as the part of a plant that attaches itself to the ground to provide support, typically underground, supplying water and nourishment to the rest of the plant. When I think of the word root, I also think of a root canal. A root canal removes the pain and saves the tooth. A root canal is normally done because of inflammation or infection in the root of the tooth.

The dentist removes the pulp inside the tooth and cleans, disinfects, and shapes the root canal by placing a filling to seal the space. Jesus is our root canal. He removes all signs of death and defeat. He cleanses us, and then he disinfects us by placing the Holy Spirit in our hearts once we are saved. We are then filled with the evidence of signs of speaking in tongues with power and authority (see Acts 2:1–4). (See note 6.)

I acknowledged my sin—called it by name. I had to be truthful and call my nakedness exactly what it was. God delivered me by my confession. The enemy cannot live inside of a believer, but he often comes to speak lies to us. He would tell me, "If you tell anyone, they are going to think negatively about you." The Word of God transformed my thinking.

> Finally, brethren, whatever things are true, whatever things are noble, whatever things are just, whatever things are pure, whatever things are lovely, whatever things are of good report, if there is any virtue and if there is anything praiseworthy—meditate on these things. (Philippians 4:8)

Whatever is going on in your mind, baby, strip it off before you process it as normal thinking (see Proverbs 23:7). I believed that I was no longer in bondage, and the power it had over me was gone.

I asked God to show me myself. I built a relationship with God—intimacy. This was easy because I knew about being intimate (but not in a godly way). I did not know the difference between a good man and a godly man. I told God exactly how I felt. I would share things with Him, and He would give me a word back. During this time, I became an intercessor as I built my prayer life.

How Badly Do You Want to Be Free?

I was sick of me. When I thought of my sin, I wanted to vomit. In the Bible, Tamar did not stand around with a "woe is me" attitude; neither should we. We have to remove excuses when we talk about getting free. Tamar moved away from the situation because of shame. I had no shame because I was selfish. It was all about me.

Wanting to be free is dealing with yourself. I was tired of me. Until you get tired of being tied up and tangled up, you will not be free. You will stay in bondage, looking for someone to feel sorry for you. I do not feel sorry for you or me. You have to make a choice. It is up to you to make some new decisions, starting today.

When will you move away from the situation? Will you stand around making excuses? Will you wait until you have AIDS or

HIV? Or will you wait until life has beat you down and you want to commit suicide?

Take time with yourself. Do something different. I do not want to be like the teapot sitting on the stove that whistles, but when the water is poured out, it is only lukewarm. I want to be hot to set things on fire in my life first (see 1 Corinthians 9:27). People do not want to only hear what you have to say; they want to see the fruit of what you are saying.

I said, "Michele has to go in order for Michele to be free!" Freedom comes at a cost, but I willingly untied myself from the strongholds since Jesus paid it all for my freedom. I owe no man for this freedom but God. I am determined to fight for my freedom. I am willing to lose my life to be free of me. I have enslaved myself too long. Today I choose to be free of Michele.

Why I Never Felt Shame

I never felt shame because I was selfish. Imagine lifting weights in the gym for the first time. Initially, the weight is heavy, but as you continue to lift, the weight becomes normal. Adding weight is necessary to feel the grip and the pain. I never felt the pain of sin because it had become normal to me.

The world calls crazy normal. Nothing about my actions were normal.

I did not feel the shame to know it was wrong, but I knew the hurt.

> I thought, "Surely she'll honor me now, accept my discipline and correction, find a way of escape from the trouble she's in, find relief from the punishment I'm bringing." But it didn't faze her. Bright and early she was up at it again, doing the same old things. (Zephaniah 3:7, The Message Bible)

I knew no shame, humiliation, guilt, or wrong feelings for my foolish behavior. God sent me warning after warning, but I refused to listen. I thank God that His mercy endures forever.

Sin was like showering and getting dressed. Sin became my everyday wear. Wherever I went, I took it with me. My muscles had learned how to lift the sin.

When God became my personal trainer, He told me that I was going to have to put down the old barbells. He told me that I was going to have to lift weights until I felt the weight of it—the pain, shame, and regret. I started to feel the weight of the sin. When God showed me myself in the mirror, I felt shame. The weight was not Michele's weight. It was something different.

Sometimes, depending on your weight, you may not like going to the gym at peak times because you feel self-conscious or wonder who is watching. The purpose of a personal trainer is to have someone to demonstrate exercises and routines, assist in exercises to minimize injuries and promote fitness, monitor progress, and provide information and resources on general fitness and health issues. (See note 7.)

My Personal Trainer told me to lift Hebrews 12:1, "Therefore we also, since we are surrounded by so great a cloud of witnesses, let us lay aside every weight, and the sin which so easily ensnares us, and let us run with endurance the race that is set before us."

As I was running this race, I told God that I needed to take a break, a day off. He told me that the race I was getting ready to run was not given to the swift nor the strong but the one who endures to the end (see Ecclesiastes 9:11). I needed to build my muscles up because I was weak in the area of my sin. I had no power or authority. I sinned for so long because it was a part of who I was.

God pushed me to limits that I never thought possible. God rebuilt my muscle; it was no longer just fat. The repetition of reading God's Word daily made me stronger, just as doing reps with weights builds physical muscles. God's Word pushed me to the next level of my life.

The Naked Truth
*****

The first thing you have to do is admit that you
are naked. Do not lie to yourself about you.

Michele's Heart
*****

Thank You, God, for removing the chains of bondage. We
want You more than we want ourselves. We are desperate for You
to deliver us from our past and start new beginnings. Thank You,
Father, that we did not get what we deserved while we were on
borrowed time. Thank You that You exposed the sin and we have
come to a place to acknowledge the sin that we deal with. We change
places with our old nature, and we call forth the new.

Exposing the Lies
Daydreams always come true.

3. Your fantasy life is attainable. People will always give you what you want when you want it.

For in the multitude of dreams and many words
there is also vanity. But fear God.
—Ecclesiastes 5:7

CHAPTER 3

The Plastic Barbie and Ken

Plastic is a substance or material that can be easily shaped or molded. When I was a child, my Barbie and Ken, female and male plastic dolls, were my favorite toys. However, I allowed something normally used to hold trash (plastic) to shape my thinking about life. I built the foundation of my understanding of love and relationships through my wild imagination and two lifeless figures.

Barbie, fashioned by Mattel, has a beautifully designed head, covered with perfect hair but without a brain—not a thing for her to consider. Barbie did not desire to be like me, but I dreamed about becoming Barbie all of the time (so much so, I must include this chapter). Truthfully, the only thing Barbie and I had in common was the fact in 1968, the first black Barbie doll made her debut, and I was also born that same year. (See note 8.)

I played with my dolls until I was about thirteen years old. My Barbie always had the best doll clothes, cars, dollhouse, and husband, Ken. This was a fairy tale that I hoped one day would become my reality. I lived in a fantasy world of becoming Barbie because there was no one telling me no. My fantasy was my reality but a very dysfunctional reality. If I wanted it, I could have it, no matter the cost or who was hurt in that process.

> I charge you, O daughters of Jerusalem, Do not
> stir up nor awaken love until it pleases.
> —Song of Solomon 8:4

What Is Your Reality?

Barbie was nice to Ken, so they never argued in my fantasy world. In reality, I talked too much, cussed, and yelled all of the time (before accepting Christ). I did not know how to communicate properly because I played with plastic dolls for so long. When it is make-believe, everything is always perfect. I played the plastic-doll role to its limits.

I had to tell myself, "Michele, wake up. Michele, snap out of it! In real life, you have to cook, clean, work, and pay bills in order to live." I never learned how to cook growing up. When I played, my Barbie doll sat down for dinner together with Ken and the kids. The food preparation was never a problem for Barbie. Barbie never had flour in her hair or sauces spilled on her clothes. Personally, I was missing too many details in a role as a wife (or girlfriend), so I made it up as I went along.

In our world, we cannot expect things to just happen for the family—not like my plastic world. Somebody has to work and train the kids. Paul exhorted the Thessalonians, "If anyone will not work, neither shall he eat" (2 Thessalonians 3:10). During playtime, I decided what I wanted for my Barbie, not realizing that my life was going to be very different from my dreams.

I did not see a husband and wife in my home. Most children have mother and father role models in their home. My dad did not live with us, but I always had a stepfather or one of my mom's boyfriends around. I formulated an idea of what intimacy is, or what I wanted it to be for me.

My playhouse experience became more and more of a reality as a young teenager taking care of other little people. In my mind, babysitting my nieces allowed me to take on the role of Barbie. I did not realize the difference between the real people and plastic dolls. With a childlike mind, I combed their hair and dressed them in order to take them outside to play. As children, this is what we do—play and imagine. I was very selfish in my thinking. Please note, when you play "house," that is exactly what you are doing, just playing house. In my role of Barbie, as a little girl, I never thought about what Ken wanted or asked him how he felt about anything.

It Is Not Supposed to Be Like This

My Ken doll qualifications had to be a tough guy, someone who could protect me. I had a relationship with "Ken," searching for the one that would give me all that I had dreamed of with my Barbie dolls. Unfortunately, I had several pregnancies that turned into abortions. My dreams quickly ended as I dealt with the reality of my relationships.

Prior to being married, I believed I could use my body to get what I wanted. I did not like public transportation growing up because I never felt safe. I learned how to hitchhike. It was dangerous, but while living on the edge, it really did not matter. I would only get in the cars of older men because at that time, I thought if they tried something, I could probably take them out.

I would give some of the older gentleman my number or take theirs because I had a plan for them too. I would use these older men to take me where I needed to go and as my sugar daddies for weekend fun. There was no sex involved, but I would go to dinner or just hang out from time to time to get their money. Remember my fantasy as Barbie … Barbie got whatever Barbie wanted.

I started smoking cigarettes. This was not something my fantasy Barbie and Ken did during my playtime. I saw others smoking, and I decided to give it a try. I never developed a drug habit growing up but tried it a couple of times. Drugs were definitely not for me. I felt out of control like a zombie; my status in life was to be in control, and I did not like the feeling of not being in control of my feelings and emotions.

On one occasion, I was getting high and I did not know the drugs had been laced with something. While in the kitchen making pancakes, I threw the batter up on the ceiling to see if it would stick; instead, it dripped all over me. I realized that getting high was not for me. I also realized that some things had to change in my life.

Trading Fantasy for Reality

I decided to move far away from my fantasy life. Past hurts that are not dealt with will always cause problems in future relationships. I would like to remind you I am a daddy's girl. I am used to getting whatever I want and having it my way. The Barbie that I had fantasized about in my mind all those years took over my life.

My man was supposed to be like the plastic Ken, handsome, driving a nice car, taking care of me financially, and coming straight home from work to me and the kids. We were never supposed to have any problems.

When I married Tim, I thought I could do whatever I wanted, and he would buy me what I wanted and just take care of me without a second thought. I felt like the real Barbie because I was the stay-at-home mom and shopped whenever I wanted to, even when I did not have the money. It is called buy now, pay later—credit cards (defined as stupidity when this strategy is used irresponsibly, leading you straight to the poorhouse and bad credit). Whatever I wanted to do, I did just that.

I tried to fit Tim into my plastic Ken's role. I never thought about his feelings. In my imagination, I could pick and choose whatever I wanted out of life. I easily accepted the good and never dealt with the bad; however, I had to learn that I needed both.

Casting Down Imaginations

The Bible teaches us in 2 Corinthians 10:5, "Casting down imaginations, and every high thing that exalteth itself against the knowledge of God, and bringing into captivity every thought to the obedience of Christ" (KJV). If we do not apply this to our lives, wrong imaginations can become a stronghold. It is necessary to be mindful of our children and their imaginations. Little girls love doll babies, but we must make sure they are playing with them as just doll babies.

A period of fantasy and living a lifestyle of fornication led to adultery because I did not control my imaginations or my thought life.

During this season of my life, when I dealt carelessly with my imagination, I would return to my old lifestyle. As I reminisced about past encounters, the enemy would use strategies to bait me and convince me to repeat a pattern of sin. I committed adultery again and again because I continued to think about the sin of my past.

How do you control what you are thinking about or imagining in your mind? Worship music, reading scripture, or just talking it out with someone who will hold you accountable will keep you from returning to the place I have named Stuck. If you do not replace the imaginations, you will remain in the same unhealthy place in your life.

Changing your mind and the things you think about is of vital importance because you have what you consider (see Proverbs 23:7). I recommend that you deal with your thoughts quickly, whether they are good or bad. Do not play with your thoughts of fantasies that are not in agreement with God's Word. You will make things a reality that you should have never been pondering.

What Does Love Have to Do with It?

What does love have to do with it? *Webster's New World Dictionary* defines love as a strong affection, liking someone. Where did you learn about love? Did you see love growing up in your home? Do you have a fantasy of something you created love to be?

When you think of intimacy and love, do you think of having sex? Did he take me to dinner or hold my hand? Do you think of affection? When I talk about older men and spending their money,

I was loving myself, getting what I wanted. What does love have to do with you?

Again, I ask, "Do you love yourself?" If you love yourself, you will not allow anyone to treat you any kind of way. In abusive relationships, women often say, "But he loves me," or when he cheats on you and you say, "But he loves me." That is not love.

From my experience, I tied love to the wrong things, such as, "How does he make me feel?" or "Did he come home at night?" Let me just be clear. I stayed (physically present) in relationships, but mentally I was long gone. Things have really gone too far when you disregard the fact he has a chick on the side.

First of all, you have to love you! Define what love is to you. You cannot give love if you do not love yourself. You have to love yourself enough to say that you are not going to take anything that you do not deserve. As husband and wife, you will have to make a healthy compromise in your relationship. This is based upon two different people from two walks of life trying to live in one space.

You should never compromise who you are just to have a man or to be able to say that someone loves you. Both males and females sometimes compromise because they hear the word *love*. What do you say love is? Only you can define what love is to you. Please understand there is a difference between "I love you" and "I am in love with you."

"For this reason a man shall leave his father and mother and be joined to his wife, and the two shall become one flesh" (Ephesians 5:31).

I have learned the following: (1) that "I am in love with you" means I must love Michele unconditionally and others; (2) I am willing to forgive you in spite of the hurt you may have caused me; and (3) I do not have to be right all the time, and in humility, I can say that I am sorry.

What Are You Willing to Do to Love You First?

You should not go into a relationship before loving yourself first. If you try this, you will only change partners without changing the behavior. This is a relationship pattern that will never work. If you want something different, you have to do something different. I say these things to myself daily: "You are beautiful. You deserve to be happy. You are an original. Do not try to be a duplicate of anyone else. Michele is fabulous. Why? Because I love me first!"

Are you willing to pay a price or be the price that is paid? Love cost Jesus His life. What are you willing to pay to love yourself? Change your behavior, change your mind, and change your life. If you love yourself, today is the day that you die to your selfish ways. I love me enough today to repent about my actions and go to God with my whole heart.

You cannot put a value on love. Are you a dime, a dollar, or that millionaire woman who believes you are worth more than that? It is beyond money, but we equate everything in life to money. When we talk about being free, I am willing to pay whatever it takes. I will walk, crawl, scream, or fight to get my freedom; I want love just as much. I have to be willing to put out as much as I want to receive.

Love is selfless. I have learned to serve my husband. I often tell people how much he loves me. Today, we are on an equal playing field (if not even more, in terms of how much I love him). There was a time that I did not love him. I did not value him or respect him. I would belittle him with my mouth.

I never put my hands on him. I am sure there were times that he would have preferred that I hit him. Our words carry weight and power. We can use our words to build up or tear down. Today I choose to build my man and my marriage to be all that God intends marriage to become.

There were times that I said things to my husband, and he could have believed that I hated him. My mouth was so reckless. I am now willing to put forth work, time, energy, and effort. I am willing to sacrifice for him because I love him. No man compares to him. Tim is my "apple scrapple."

My love for Tim is undeniable because I love him on purpose. I am determined to love him the way he deserves to be loved, and that is not based on how I feel. News break: our feelings lie to us often, but true love goes beyond our feelings.

I had to learn to replace the heavy weight of my words with healthy conversation, which we now call "pillow talk." I encourage all married couples to find time to have pillow talk; it is a necessary element in your love for each other. Tim and I get in bed with the grapes and good conversation. We bless the Lord for whatever it leads to!

Supply and Demand

The plastic dolls created a world in my mind that every little girl dreams about. Unfortunately, the fantasy did not teach me about the supply and demands of life. However, God supplied for each of us before there was ever any demand. My parents supplied the dolls, but I did not see how they did so; I only knew that I had the supplies as I demanded them (respectfully).

I put demands on life that were not realistic. I started losing in my real world before it ever got started. Stop setting yourself up for failure because you have not planned properly. God did not try to figure out what He wanted to do with humankind after Adam sinned. God is the creator of life; He had our supply prepared in Jesus Christ. As I was building a fantasy life with my dolls, God had already supplied a better life for me (see Phil 4:19). Will you accept Him today?

The Naked Truth
*****

Do not allow what Mattel created as a plastic toy for kids to define your life story. Wake up and deal with your reality!

Michele's Heart
*****

Father, we thank You right now in the name of Jesus. We cannot cut anything with plastic, and that is all that Barbie and Ken were. Thank You that we are going to sharpen each other and come out as pure gold. The fantasies in our minds that have become demonic strongholds, we tear them down in the name of Jesus. We submit our will to Your will. We deny ourselves. We want to walk with You and talk to You. We have learned over the years what we thought love was, but it was a fantasy. Thank You for showing us what true love is. We will not love with strings attached. Help those who have been hurt to love again!

Exposing the Lies
You got the power!

4. You can have anybody you want. Just take them!

So David's anger was greatly aroused against the man, and he said
to Nathan, "As the Lord lives, the man who has done this shall
surely die! And he shall restore fourfold for the lamb, because he
did this thing and because he had no pity." Then Nathan said to
David, "You are the man! Thus says the Lord God of Israel: 'I
anointed you king over Israel, and I delivered you from the hand of
Saul. I gave you your master's house and your master's wives into
your keeping, and gave you the house of Israel and Judah. And
if that had been too little, I also would have given you more!'"
—2 Samuel 12:5–9

CHAPTER 4

Takers

Takers—someone who always takes from others but never gives back. You cannot always give in the same level someone gives to you, but you can at least say thank you. Gratitude costs you nothing and takes nothing from you as an individual. I was not raised to always take but to help others in need. It is more blessed to give than to receive (see Acts 20:35). My prayer is that I give more than I take.

"Now it came to pass in the evening, that he took Leah his daughter and brought her to Jacob; and he went in to her" (Genesis 29:23).

Many people blame Laban, but from a woman's perspective, Leah knew exactly what she was doing to Rachel. Women can be very possessive of what another person has. Just because it looks good does not mean it is good for you. It is hard to believe that any woman would give birth to several children with a man she did not plan to spend her life with—especially for Leah. Seeing that she was unloved, the Lord opened her womb (Genesis 29:31).

Laban had a part in this game. He was using his daughters for his own gain. If you are considering the culture during that time, you may be thinking Leah may not have had a choice in the relationship. However, let us take a look at the names and what Leah said when she gave birth to her children.

Rueben—"The Lord has surely looked on my affliction. Now therefore, my husband will love me" (Genesis 29:32).

Simeon—"Because the Lord has heard that I am unloved, He has therefore given me this son also" (Genesis 29:33).

Levi—"Now this time my husband will become attached to me, because I have borne him three sons" (Genesis 29:34).

Judah—"Now I will praise the Lord" (Genesis 29:35).

Issachar – "God has given me my wages, because I have given my maid to my husband" (Genesis 30:18).

Zebulun—"God has endowed me with a good endowment; now my husband will dwell with me, because I have borne him six sons" (Genesis 30:19).

Leah also had a daughter named Dinah.

I did not have the children but understood firsthand how to play the game. Leah had learned to play the game too. Leah took the challenge to gamble. She knew that Jacob loved her sister and that he was going to work seven years for her. I gambled with my life while knowing that what you sow you will reap.

The following thoughts are reckless: *If I have his baby, surely he will be with me, or at least he is going to be a part of my life.* This is how some men become labeled as a "baby daddy." Personally, I feel too many women fall into this trap of "If I have his baby …" It is not true at all.

After having my oldest daughter, she became my primary focus, and I knew she was going to have a better life than what I had. I decided if I was going to do bad, I would do bad all by myself. At times, I could not see the bad because I never lacked any material thing. At that time in my life, in comparison to my friends, I was doing pretty well for myself.

Leah was just like me. I was going to work the player while hating the game. I hated what I had to do at times to stay in the game, but I was not willing to get disqualified. Like Leah, I believed since he kept coming to me, I had a chance. Thank God it did not take me having six children to realize that I needed to take my dignity back. I was not going to be just another baby mama.

Leah had game also. Her behavior demonstrated that two can play this game. I believe she named her children with a plan in the back of her mind that she could one day take Jacob from Rachel. Takers never win. Jacob loved Rachel, and love is always the glue that holds the relationship together.

Living the Life of a Taker

I love the movie *Takers*. It is about a group of bank robbers who found their multimillion-dollar plan, but it was interrupted by a determined detective. This movie was right up my alley, with fine gentlemen who had a lot of swagger. They played the part of my Ken; they had money, cars, and nice houses and were smart businessmen. However, they were not satisfied with what they had. Greed set in because takers always want more than what they have.

I have read about rich people taking their lives because money is not the answer to all things. Today, I could live in a box with my husband because we have contentment. I am not saying I would like it, but I know what it feels like to be misplaced in life. There are just some things money cannot buy, and true love is one of them. When you love a person, you are showing selflessness.

I played the role of a taker for a season in my life. I had a very seductive spirit and the attitude to match it. This is not what God had for me, but I wanted to do things my way. I did not want God anywhere in the equation in this part of my life. This type of attitude really caused a lot of hurt to my family as well as other families.

I told a lot of lies to my family about where I was going. I even told my husband I was enrolled in school to have the flexibility of being out of the house without being questioned. Please hear me.

Takers are only concerned about themselves. I did not care who I hurt as long as I was getting what I wanted, when I wanted it.

As a taker, I learned to believe my lies because it sounded real. It is a shame when you tell a lie so long until it becomes your truth. I was so crazy I believed it.

Takers will come in and wreck your home. It did not matter if the man was married with kids or in a relationship. I had the "don't care" attitude. I learned how to become a taker and enjoyed being a taker. So sad. It did not matter that some of these men had children. To take from a child like this, I equate it to driving drunk.

Before a person takes that first drink, they know it is a possibility that they may get drunk. If that person does not care, they drink anyway. Then they have the nerve to get behind the wheel of a car, knowing they are under the influence of alcohol. Oftentimes, they get into an accident and kill someone.

During those years that I spent being a taker, I was no different than a drunk driver to many homes. Homes were dying at my hand due to my careless attitude. When children grow up in a broken home, they suffocate. They feel like daddy or mommy has time for everything but them, so rejection sets in.

Stuck on Me

Stuck on me was like being stuck on stupid. I remember one time I got stuck on an elevator. I started breathing heavily, sweating, and getting nervous. This was an older elevator in an apartment building filled with people. It was only three minutes, but it felt like a lifetime. Understand that the decisions you make today, good or bad, you will be stuck with the consequences for the rest of your life. Food for thought: can you live with your decisions?

I was able to get out of the elevator, but the anxiety that I had in those few minutes was something I never want to feel again. Will you be fortunate enough to get out? Do not gamble with your life because you are like I was—stuck on stupid. Stop listening to people who do not even like you. People tell you what you should do, but they are not even doing what they are telling you to do. There is nothing wrong with a second opinion. Many people have not had to have surgery due to a second opinion.

Be careful who you keep company with. Do not share all of your business with everyone. Everyone may not be happy for you. Do not be deceived. Bad company corrupts good character. (See 1 Corinthians 15:33.)

My best friend and I loved going to the Go-Go's to see Chuck Brown. She was a hairstylist, and she would do hair all day just to make sure she had enough money to buy us matching outfits to go out on the town. I was so sure of myself that I would "book somebody" when we went out. I was always dressed to kill from head to toe. She was my Barbie personal stylist, so if a Ken showed up on the scene, he would be impressed.

I was not ready to yield to the will of the Father. I continued to allow my flesh to speak for and through me.

"For those who are living according to the flesh set their minds on the things of the flesh [which gratify the body]" (Romans 8:5, Amplified Bible).

Reflection

As I reflect, I was like Jezebel when she told Ahab she would get him the vineyard he wanted from Naboth (see 1 Kings 21). We always joked about women having the Jezebel spirit and tied it to women who wore red lipstick. Jezebel was possessive and took matters into her own hands. Jezebel arranged Naboth's murder. I have never killed anyone, but I have done things that have caused marriages to end and relationships to be broken.

I never thought about the cost of a home being torn apart. Tim suffered many disappointments and times of depression because of my actions. I often thought to myself, *How did I get here again?* If the truth be told, it happened one bad decision after another.

A taker is never happy. I was married with my *own* husband ... the flesh is never satisfied. This attitude is so much more than a "hot night in the sheets." I did not have the joy of intimacy while I was sleeping around. The thrill was making that married man lie to his wife just to get out of the house. The power move of encouraging that boyfriend to tell his girlfriend he had to go out of town just to be with me for the weekend. When you think of the word *take*, it always takes away—never adding value.

It took me from my Tim and him being my only lover after marriage. I went from being a fornicator to becoming an adulteress. I did not just take from other homes, I took me from my children. There were nights I should have been home helping them with homework, cooking, or just being there to help raise them. Actually, I did not take anyone's man. I took myself away from raising my children up in the way they should go (see Proverbs 22:6).

Sex has an attitude, and it is nasty outside of marriage. When role playing (like husband and wife) prior to marriage, we come into the relationship with all kinds of spirits. I did not understand the difference between lust and sex and how God intended for sex at its highest level of intimacy to be between husband and wife. Prior to a Christ-filled life, I was fulfilling the lust of my flesh.

I have given you a few things that I did in my life up to this point. I want you to understand that every man you lie down with, you get up with a part of him. It may be his smell that you walk away and carry with you throughout the day or whatever troubles he may be going through. These things are known as soul ties.

To any of my readers that may have experienced this pain in their life or by me personally, I ask for your forgiveness. God has forgiven me, and I had to learn to forgive myself.

Counterfeit Living

Let's talk about how I misused my powers as a woman. This power is like money that you mismanage, leaving you broke. When you misuse the power that has been given to you, you are like counterfeit money. One of the ways counterfeit bills can be detected is the color-shifting ink. The twenty-dollar bill is most commonly counterfeited.

As of 1996, all bills five dollars and greater have a security feature. The twenty-dollar bill, on the bottom right-hand corner, has a copper color when looking straight at it. If you rotate the bill, it is easier on the eyes and has more of a greenish color. Looking back at some of my pictures, my skin was darker because I was living a counterfeit life. Now that I have changed my life and am living the real deal, my skin is much lighter. (See note 9.)

Bank robbers do not *ask* the clerk at the counter for money. Robbers demand that money be put into the bags, "Now!" Thieves do not ask, "Can I come into your house and steal your stuff?" They come when you are not home and take your stuff.

"Most assuredly, I say to you, he who does not enter the sheepfold by the door, but climbs up some other way, the same is a thief and a robber" (John 10:1).

The enemy's job was to take me down and destroy me before I became who God designed me to be. If you allow him, he will take your peace without your consent. I decided to take back my family, money, life, and image from Satan. I told him he could steal no more.

Take your dreams back. You are not a failure but a conqueror in Christ Jesus. I had to learn that no one, not even Satan, can take anything from me unless I allow it. Now I choose to take the Word of God and live!

In life, there are consequences to everything good or bad.
If you are a taker, you must be willing to pay the price.

Grace and Mercy

Thank God for His grace and mercy. I had a good friend and sister who died from AIDS. She was not out there sleeping around, but God showed me through her death that His hand was on me. I also thank God for the praying husband that He gave me, Timothy Wayne Turner Sr.

I pray that this chapter causes you to think about others. I had to learn to value and respect others. How other people feel does matter to me. I would never want what I have done to others to happen to me. I have been gracefully broken. I have not reaped what I have sown. Thank You, Lord, for crop failure.

> We are not here to take sides but to take
> over as believers in Jesus Christ.
> —Dr. Bill Winston

The Naked Truth
*****

Handle people just how you want to be handled—with care!

Michele's Heart
*****

Father, I thank You for deliverance. I thank You that I no longer desire to take from myself or others. Thank You, God, that I have not slept with another man other than my husband since 1999. You have shown me how to love my husband. I pray for healing in marriages where there has been infidelity. I pray we beat our bodies into submission according to Your Word. I come against that foul spirit of lust, fornication, and adultery. I pray for women to be whole in mind, body, and soul. In Jesus's name. Amen.

Exposing the Lies
You cannot overcome infidelity in your marriage.

5. You will never find a good man. Living the single life is not that bad.

Marriage *is* honorable among all, and the bed undefiled;
but fornicators and adulterers God will judge.
—Hebrews 13:4

CHAPTER 5

He Married Me Anyway

Then Boaz said to his servant who was in charge of the
reapers, "Whose young woman is this?" —Ruth 2:5

In the Bible, Boaz gave Ruth favor and respect. He instructed the
young men in the field to purposely leave grain for Ruth to pick up
(see Ruth 2:16). The same is true with Tim. He has always covered
me, taking better care of me than I did of myself. My behavior gave
Tim a right to call me out of my name, but he never did so. For me,
Tim is an example of the true love of the Father here on earth.

Here Comes the Bride

Here comes the bride. People all over the world spend thousands
and even millions of dollars on their wedding. I did not. Tim and
I were married at the Marine Corps Base Chapel, Cherry Point,
North Carolina. Whether you go to the justice of the peace, a chapel,

or a destination wedding, be ready to say "I do" for all the right reasons. I did not. It cost me major problems later.

As I walked down the aisle, I never thought about making my wedding vows unto God or loving Tim "until death do us part." I thought of both my sisters, appearing happily married to Marines. Both of them had more than what I knew a husband to be.

As I look back at our wedding picture, I am amazed that Tim actually married me. Tim had been engaged to two other women prior to me. What made him want to give up those other women for me? Only Tim could answer that question, so I had to ask him. Tim answered by saying, "I knew you were the one for me. I was ready to settle down and have kids, and I knew I wanted you to be with me for the rest of my life. I knew I was not perfect and felt we would be good for one another. I did not realize all that we would go through. I am glad to know that we can weather any storm together."

I began seeking the Lord for that answer, and he showed me Matthew 1:19, "Then Joseph her husband, being a just man, and not wanting to make her a public example, was minded to put her away secretly." It all made sense to me. God had given me a good man. The fact Tim joined the United States Marine Corps further proved he was one of the few good men.

Tim asked my brothers-in-law about me. He made a bet that he would win me over. He won. There was something different about him that caused me to say yes to his proposal. Tim was my Boaz, but I was not the Ruth that we read about in the scriptures. I did not need to be Ruth. I only needed to be myself; that is what drew Tim to me.

Tim knew that there was something more inside of me. I have learned there is no man more loving and understanding than Timothy Wayne Turner Sr. I cheated on Tim as his girlfriend. He should have run in another direction. However, we were married on November 14, 1987, saying our I do's anyway. In all truth, I cannot say that we married for love.

Tim is a *what you see is what you get* kind of guy. He is faithful, loving, and kind and truly demonstrates longsuffering. The fruit of the spirit is definitely a part of his character. I could write an entire book containing all of the many wonderful things about him. Tim has not been perfect, but he has worn his armor like a Marine. I honor marriage now, for my eyes have been enlightened to the true meaning. I see Tim as the king that he is. This man has blown my mind by how much he loves me.

What God Joins Together

The marriage in the Bible that I identify most with is found in the book of Hosea:

> When the Lord began to speak by Hosea, the Lord said to Hosea:
> "Go, take yourself a wife of harlotry and children of harlotry, for the land has committed great harlotry by departing from the Lord." (Hosea 1:2)

Hosea

Why would a loving God tell Hosea to marry a prostitute? The book of Hosea demonstrates the relationship of God and Israel through the life of Hosea and his wife, Gomer—a harlot. God is filled with wisdom and knows how to get our attention. God spoke with Tim just as he had spoken with Hosea.

I know Tim had thoughts in the back of his mind that I would one day bring him disappointment. I am glad his attraction toward me was greater than his fears. Someone once said fear is *f*alse *e*vidence *a*ppearing *r*eal.

The history of my behavior always had Tim wondering, *What if?* I am glad my evidence did not have a grip on Tim loving me again. At this point, it has been more than twenty years, and I pray there are no doubts in Tim's mind.

I will speak for me. Fear is not of God, and I have the authority to speak a thing, and it shall be so. If I have not been anything, I have been consistently faithful to God first. I have learned to respect myself and my husband. There is nothing false about me; I am the real Michele.

"God has not given us a spirit of fear" (2 Timothy 1:7). Real men do cry, and they do not quit! That is my Timothy W. Turner Sr., a true man of God.

God's love is unconditional even when we are not deserving. The prophet Jeremiah records, "'Return, O backsliding children,' says the Lord, 'for I am married to you'" (Jeremiah 3:14). The story of Hosea offers hope and restoration after true repentance. Hosea captures the love of God for His people.

It is amazing to know that the all-wise God can love you, but it is a feeling of gratitude when a human can love someone like me. We do not always have the grace for one another's mistakes.

I cannot say that God told Tim I would act like a prostitute. However, can someone say, "Praise God for Timothy W. Turner Sr.?" In those early years, I thought Tim was a weak man for allowing my infidelity. Other men may have chosen to divorce me or to go upside my head. Tim did neither. He spoke with a lawyer but realized divorce was not God's plan for us. There is nothing weak about Tim. He is a very strong man with a lot of patience.

In today's society, the man is normally known as the one who cheats. It takes a real man to stay with his wife and allow her to tell the whole world the things she did and still be able to walk around with his head and pride intact. I know he prayed a lot. He valued our marriage commitment and refused to become another statistic. He often told me that he would not abort his family. He did not want to be like his dad, who walked out on his mom and his brothers when he was just a kid.

The book of Hosea is powerful to me because it describes my marriage with Tim. Gomer and Hosea's marriage was restored, just as God would reconcile with His people. God used a bad marriage to show the world what happens when two people allow Him to be the Lord of their lives.

Just because it is bad does not mean it is over. I had to get my head and body together. Do you not know that your head can take your body places it does not want to go? I had to change my way of thinking about what I thought about. I saw my husband in a different light as he served the Lord. It made me say, "I am missing out on something." Today, God has given us the ministry of reconciliation (see 2 Corinthians 5:18). God has reconciled our hearts and minds to become as one.

Misbehaving

Tim was an active-duty Marine when we married. Within twelve months of marriage, he was deployed overseas. Our son was born during this time and was in the company of many of my male friends. Thank God he never made a connection with any male prior to Tim's return. Ever since Tim's return, ten months after he was born, their father-son bond has been so special.

My failure to conduct myself as Tim's wife due to his absence was not a license for me to commit adultery. My husband was serving our country and providing for our home. I was guilty of my misconduct for years, but I realized I was very immature and stubborn. My bad behavior led to many bad decisions.

Tim has caught me in hotels, at the homes of other men, and with guys at my mom's house. My family has always loved Tim and believed he was God sent. My family never turned their backs on me, and I thank them for that. They told me that I was wrong, but they understood that I was a grown woman making my own decisions.

I had to change my behavior in order to change my life. God saves us, but we have free will. I had to decide whether I was going to continue on with this foolish behavior or rise to the occasion of being a wife and mother. You can take a deer to the water, but you cannot make him drink.

Get Up and Live

The final relationship I was involved in led me to encounter the Holy Spirit like never before. One night, I felt the Holy Spirit say to me, "You better get up out of this relationship or you are going to die and go to hell!" I tried to reason with the Lord. I said, "Lord, hell, where there's gnashing of teeth?" His response was, "Yes!"

I knew I was bad but not bad enough to end up in hell. By this time, I had become pregnant. I called Tim and asked him if I could come home. Although he said yes, I had to let him know that I was with child. Tim reminded me that he had already raised a child from my previous relationship. I decided to have an abortion.

Today, I do not believe in abortions because now I know better and will do better. I do not believe because I was irresponsible that I had a right to take this unborn child's life. When you live a life of sin, it affects everyone, without them having a choice in the matter.

Going Home

Moving back home was the easy part for me. My struggle was dealing with my thoughts. Tim would come home from work and find me in my closet, wailing and crying. My flesh and my spirt were warring against each other. Tim would tell our children, "Mommy is going through a process, but she will be okay." I found deliverance by starving my flesh and feeding my spirit. I had allowed my flesh to rule for too long.

I started reading my Bible every day. I learned how to rebuke myself ... I was fighting against myself. I allowed the Word to help me fight. The flesh wanted to go back into that lifestyle, but my spirit won the battle.

In the book of Proverbs, God's Word began to speak to me about my life. Each time Tim deployed overseas, I became the immoral woman described in Proverbs 7:19, "For my husband is not at home; he has gone on a long journey."

Most people would have chosen to divorce if the spouse had cheated for ten years. But God knew we would serve Him with our whole heart once the strongholds of pride, selfishness, and unforgiveness were broken. We do not believe in divorce because we are a product of what God can and will do if we put our marriage in His hand. We had to yield to the plans of the Father for our marriage. We stood on God's promise to deliver me from the lifestyle of adultery.

Renewed and Restored

We renewed our vows on November 12, 2005. I finally had my dream wedding. We wrote our vows to each other. Prior to the wedding, we fasted for thirty days without sexual intimacy. I had my first bridal shower. During the wedding reception, I washed his feet as a token of my love. I wanted to show Tim how much he meant to me and that I was willing to humble myself for him. Washing his feet was a small thing to do compared to how much he has done for me.

Our honeymoon was on a cruise ship to the Bahamas. This was the honeymoon we never had. We wanted to do things differently than the first time we said, "I do." To every bride to be: it is not about the wedding day but every day after that day.

The salt covenant was a blessing to our wedding ceremony. Both of us took our individual bag of salt and poured it into one bag. Our salt grains are forever mixed and impossible to separate. Salt is used as a preservative. Therefore, it was an appropriate symbol for eternity. Our covenant of salt cannot be changed (see 2 Chronicles 13:5). Tim is stuck with me, as I am with him. God intended for marriages to stay together, just like the mixture of our bag of salt.

These are benefits in the kingdom when we put work into our marriage: restoration, love, trust, honesty, and faithfulness.

Whether we are saved or not when we get married, the wedding vows are pretty much the same—as unto God. Again, I emphasize, the difference is, as believers, we *do not* believe in divorce.

> Now to the married I command, *yet* not I but the Lord: A wife is not to depart from *her* husband. But even if she does depart, let her remain unmarried or be reconciled to *her* husband. And a husband is not to divorce *his* wife. (1 Corinthians 7:10–11)

I can imagine all of the excuses, and you are probably ready to close the book. I am going to say this anyway because it is the truth. When we stand at the altar, many of us do not even remember what we said, only repeating what someone told us to say. I know this because at our first wedding, I did just that.

Thank God for my opportunity to have a second chance to get it right. The second time, not only can I remember what I said, I meant it!

God has restored our marriage, and we believe in giving back. In 2007, we encountered so many marriages going through trials. We allowed God to use our marriage as a platform for those who needed hope.

God has now given us the ministry of Repairer of the Breach:

> Those from among you shall build the old waste places; you shall raise up the foundations of many generations; and you shall be called the Repairer of the Breach. (Isaiah 58:12)

Tim's Vow to Michele

> Michele, I know things at first were out of hand. People that knew us would say, "I know they are not still together!" Guess what? We are still here! I know He has not brought us this far to leave us. With God on our side, anything is possible. You have given me a beautiful family. I thank you for being by my side. You are my life and my love. I am the luckiest man in the world. I will have it no other way except to spend the rest of my life with you. I love you ... still! Tim

Michele's Vow to Tim

> Tim, this day I stand before God and these people and I say I love you. I will never understand the love

you have for me, but I thank you. If we never told people what we have been through they would never know. It is because you have allowed the words of the Apostle Paul to be our testimony, "Husbands, love your wives, just as Christ also loved the church, and gave himself for her; that he might sanctify and cleanse her with the washing of water by the word, that He might present her to Himself a glorious church, not having spot or wrinkle, or any such thing, but that she should be holy and without blemish" (Ephesians 5:25–27). I love you forever!

For the husband is head of the wife, as also Christ is head of the church; and He is the Savior of the body. (Ephesians 5:23)

The Power of the Body in Marriage

The wife hath not power of her own body, but the husband: and likewise also the husband hath not power of his own body, but the wife. (1 Corinthians 7:4 KJV)

How My Behavior Affected Tim

Once on a marriage retreat with our church, I learned the hard truth of why Tim drank alcohol. We were sharing with a couple how God had blessed our marriage. Tim shared the reason he drank so much was because he had to come home and deal with me. The truth hurt, but it was his reality. I had to deal with the fact the very thing I hated about him he was doing because he did not know how to deal with me.

That day was life changing for me because I realized Tim had not only been hurt by my adultery, but he was suffering because of my verbal abuse toward him. He would get drunk to drown me out. I apologized to him and allowed for a time of healing in our marriage. This was a truth that I needed to hear because I never understood why someone who said he loved his wife and kids would drink every day.

The Gentleman

I admire that Tim is not just a forgiving person, but he likes to smile and sing! Whenever we travel, one of the things we like to do is sing songs on the road together. He loves the oldies, and he is a great singer. My favorite song that I love to hear him sing is by Gerald Levert, "Baby Hold on to Me." Last year, I heard this song on the radio and really listened to the lyrics, and it brought me to tears:

> Girl you know I'll do just about anything to see a smile upon your face. So, don't let your friends go messing with your mind (oh no). And girl you know there ain't nothing I won't do for you baby. Don't ever doubt my love cause its true. Baby hold on to me, see I'm a special kinda man that is hard to find. Told you a thousand times, baby hold on to me.

Tim is that gentleman that opens my car doors and carries my bags into the house. He is loving to everyone he comes into contact with. He is truly a servant who loves giving and helping people. I adore how he talks about me and how well we work together.

The Naked Truth
*****

Remember why you said, "I do!"

Michele's Heart
*****

Learn to appreciate and love your husband for who God created him to be. Timothy Turner Sr., I salute you today as my man of God. You complete me. I love you forever.

*****

Father, I thank You for a husband who loves his wife unconditionally. Love is patient and kind. Love is never puffed up. Thank You for a husband who is willing to carry the weight of another person for the good of the marriage, in a world where marriage no longer means until death do us part. Thank You for the Holy Spirit that was able to show me that I was headed to destruction, which would lead to hell. What the enemy meant for my bad, thank You for turning it around for my good. Amen.

In a world where marriage is viewed as a joke and vows are not sacred, I thank You for my marriage. Thank You for breathing life back into my marriage. Thank You that it is a marriage for the world to glean from and to see that You still perform miracles. Thank You for the power and will to love my husband today and to honor him as the king that he is.

I pray for every marriage, in the name of Jesus. I plead the blood against divorce. Father, heal us. Do not allow our hearts to grow cold due to hurt, pain, or shame. I thank You that greater is He that is in us than he that is in the world. We love You, Father. Turn marriages around for Your glory!

Exposing the Lies
Just attend church.

6. Why do you need to go to church anyway? They are all the same ... judging those of us enjoying the good life.

Not forsaking the assembling of ourselves together, as
is the manner of some, but exhorting one another, and
so much the more as you see the Day approaching.
—Hebrews 10:25

CHAPTER 6

More Than a Churchgoer

When I was around seven years old, my grandmother Anna Lee took me and my siblings to church. Going home and playing church was always so much fun. We sang the songs, and of course I was the lead singer. As I recall, the problem was I never read my Bible or prayed. When I became an adult, I only took my children to church on Easter and Christmas.

The Identity of a Churchgoer

I describe churchgoers as those who quickly get in and out of the church. It is unthinkable to consider that a churchgoer would serve or help out in church. They are always too busy because of things going on at home. Churchgoers never want those nosey church folks in their business. As a churchgoer, you only learn about the politics of the church.

This type never takes notes during the sermon or studies the scriptures at home. The idea of encouraging someone else is not on their mind in the least bit. Does the churchgoer not see the person sitting next to them? The truth be told, a churchgoer is putting a check on their things-to-do list. I know how they look and how they think and act. I was a churchgoer.

Looking Like a Believer

I went to church but did not live for God or obey His Word. I knew all of the formalities, such as service start times, the words to the songs, and how to look like a believer. In those early days, I gave offerings and a tithe when I needed a blessing. I prayed when life got tough or someone in the family got sick or died, but mostly, I prayed amiss. I remember giving a ten-dollar offering and asking for change.

I cried for entire church services, hoping someone would feel sorrow for the bad decisions I had made. I would go to the altar for prayer. I never did anything the man or woman of God advised me to do. Each time I went for prayer, I was so tired of me and thought that things would be different. However, I would find myself back out there doing me ... whatever I wanted to do.

As Christians, we often take God's Word too lightly. I confessed, as in Exodus 20:7, "You shall not take the name of the Lord your God in vain, for the Lord will not hold him guiltless who takes His name in vain."

I know firsthand what it is to just quote a scripture because I have done this several times in my life on a Sunday or when life got tough. I was only going through the motions. Thank God that He is so merciful and patient.

Turning Point —Learning Church Systems

Finally, in 1995, I accepted Christ as my Savior and joined a church. I went to church every day of the week. Nothing against Baptist churches, but there was a service every night. God never intended for me to be just a churchgoer. When believers come together, we each receive from one another by sharing our faith in God.

This was a turning point for me because I ended my relationship as an adulteress. I began attending services and hearing the Word of God. Seeds of God's Word were being planted in my life. Unfortunately, I would backslide after this season of learning. Thank God that He never gave up on me in all my foolishness. I always knew He was there. I simply would not surrender to Him so that He could help me.

The Bets Were Against Me

In 1999, I really got saved. I had said, "I am saved," many times before, and it would last until I got out of my situation. My friends thought my past would always mirror my future. It was my consistent track record of returning to my sin that caused them to think this way. I had been a Christian in word only, and Christ was not in my heart.

Take God seriously and do not play with Him. I have learned in my short life that your words have power. I not only live my life to be better but also for others I come into contact with. I remember when I did not have it all together.

Today, I have prayer partners and people that I am accountable to. I tell the devil, "I win, and there is nothing you can do about it!" Paul said it best when he said to the Church at Corinth, "But thanks be to God, who gives us the victory through our Lord Jesus Christ" (1 Corinthians 15:57). As Christians, we sometimes take His Word too lightly. We claim the name but live in vain.

Salvation

In the book of Romans 10:9, we learn, "That if you confess with your mouth the Lord Jesus and believe in your heart that God has raised Him from the dead, you will be saved." Unfortunately, hell is enlarging itself because people do not think they need to be saved to go to heaven. In my experience, when witnessing to people, they say, "Please do not judge me!" My response is to say what the Word of God says, "Do not judge according to appearance, but judge with righteous judgment" (John 7:24).

We are not to condemn others but convict them of their sins. I let them know that God loves them and that is why He sent His Son to die for them. When you love God in return, there should be a change of behavior and mind-set, understanding that we need a Savior. We cannot just go through the motions.

I had to allow the words out of my mouth to match my life. I refused to be a fake Christian, saying one thing and living like a heathen. My salvation is personal. Not only did Jesus purchase me with His precious blood, but He saved me out of many impossible situations. I could have died playing with other people's lives.

When I gave my heart to the Lord in 1999, I knew I wanted something different. I was not happy with the way my life was going. I really wanted this God who called me out of darkness to manifest Himself. He saved me on purpose and with a purpose.

The Test

When I stopped playing church, I truly fell in love with Jesus Christ (who is the lover of my soul). I began to worship and give God praise with all my heart. Not everyone will be happy about your deliverance, but never let anyone stop you from giving God the praise. The enemy would love to shut you up, but I praise God even more and louder! Your praise may even get you kicked out of the church. Come on, shouting John!

I told the leadership that if I could not praise God, I would leave that church. The Holy Spirit got a hold of me and said, "If you leave, I am not going with you!" Of course, I stayed another year. It was only a test. God was teaching me how to submit to leadership and be obedient. He wanted to see how well I obeyed those in authority. He checked my heart to see how serious I was since I knew how to play church so well.

Just as Simon Peter said to Jesus when many of the disciples walked away from Him, I said, "Lord, to whom shall I go?" (see John 6:68). I had decided I was not walking away from the Lord again.

Living the Life

It matters how we live our lives and how we treat people. People are paying close attention to those of us who proclaim to be Christians. As a Christian, it matters to me how I live my life in front of people and in the privacy of my home; it should be the same. It is hypocritical if our lives are not the same at all times. People are looking for answers—right, wrong, or indifferent. They want to see that the Jesus we say we love is evident in our lives.

I am no longer just a churchgoer. I am a disciple of Jesus Christ. Titles have been given to me as licensed minister and ordained deaconess. I am a woman of God first. Titles often get people caught up, causing them to focus less on those they are serving. I feel like I was a prostitute in the world; I will not be the same in the church.

It does matter which church you attend. It is easy to get caught up in the hype of the church, but God's presence is nowhere in the building. I know who I am today. I study to show myself approved, a worker that need not be ashamed (see 2 Timothy 2:15). I could attend church every day as long as the Word of God is being taught. I love praying for people and seeing the manifestation in their lives.

We are not all called to be a pastor, but we do have a duty to make sure we are not a stumbling block for others. This is why we need self-control. We have all been marked to be a light in the midst of darkness.

Jesus spoke to His disciples about offenses (see Luke 17:1–2). It matters how we live our lives as Christians, and it matters how we treat other people. The way I was living my life did not reflect the life of a Christian. People are paying more attention to how we live than we would prefer.

No One Fails on My Watch

Anyone who really knows me will agree that I do not take this statement, "No one fails on my watch," lightly. I make this statement in confidence because I do not have a friend, family member, or a stranger who will fall on my watch. The reason is I am going to hold them accountable. If they do fall, it will not be because I did not hold them accountable to the Word of God or point them to the truth. Of course, I do this in love, whether they want me to or not.

Most people who know me love it, and those who do not know me always say they needed to be told the truth. There were times I felt like I wanted to share, but people were not ready to receive what I had to say. Today, I do not care what people think about me. I wish I had people who would have been straight with me and told me about myself. Yes, my feelings would have been hurt, but a man of God once told me, "Get your feelings saved!"

We may fall down, but we can get back up! There is a difference between falling and failing. When you fall, you can get back up, brush yourself off, and continue. When you fail, you have to start over and repeat the task. I was going straight to hell in the end, but I was tormented while I was still on the earth. I had fallen and felt like I could not get up, but thanks be to God, who causes me to triumph every time (see 2 Corinthians 2:14).

I have many friends but none that I love so much that I am not willing to tell them the hard truth. I believe in exposing someone in order to save their soul, not condemning people but loving them enough to tell them the truth. Deep down inside, people really want to be told when they are wrong.

My experiences in life may have been different if someone had confronted me in my mess. I am glad that God loved me enough to send the Holy Spirit to speak directly to me. Knowing me back then, it is quite possible that I would not have listened to anyone.

For years, people would call me John the Baptist. Today, I am known as the snatcher (see Jude 1:22-23). Who is John the Baptist? He was Jesus's cousin. John was the forerunner who prepared the way for Jesus. He lived in the desert and preached a message on repentance. This is similar to a wedding and someone yelling, "The bride is coming, the bride is coming!" One day, the Groom is coming back for His bride. Will you be ready?

There are numerous ways to minister the love of God. Some of us in the church do not like the direct approach because we decide instead to mind our own business. We are gatekeepers of the House of God. Therefore, anything that comes into the House is our business.

Our Brother's Keeper

It is important that we are our brother's keeper (see Genesis 4:9). We should not have the spirit of Cain or just be a friend. God never called me to be my leader's friend. I wanted to be, but God told me, "No!" As a friend, we do not know how to tell people the truth without watering it down or lying. God never intended for us to love people more than Him. When we do, it causes us to make the Word of God of no effect in people's lives (see Mark 7:13).

Are you responsible for others falling or are you a catcher? Do you understand that you are responsible for others and not just your four and no more? I desire to see the best in all of us.

Tim served more than twenty years in the Marine Corps. We were watching a movie together, and at the end, the fallen soldiers' faces were displayed next to their grave sites. I could see tears roll down his face. I felt in my spirit what he went through during his service to our country.

I have friends and family who have fallen away from God. When I was in my mess, I had no one to pull me out or care about what I was going through. People knew, but no one really took the time to be "my brother's keeper." In 2020, we feel like we have to mind our own business, due to unknown danger because of the state of mind of others.

We all have a civil duty. "See something, we say something." We do not want to be a stumbling block for others by judging their behavior. We must use discernment and self-control when speaking to our brothers and sisters.

Michele's Vision of the Church

I walked into what we call a church, but really it is nothing but a building. I felt like I was going into a concert because it was lights, camera, and action! I saw the doors of the sanctuary, the stage, and the people. I was seated and waiting for the show to begin. The music was magical, and the Word was entertaining, but God was not there. I got goose bumps, but that is not God.

I think we forget to invite Him into our services and allow Him to have His way. He is there because we bring Him with us, but He will not just take over. He is a gentleman. He responds the same as someone I have welcomed into my home. That person will not go into my purse and take my money out or open my refrigerator without asking. The Holy Spirit is our Helper.

We think because we've got church down to how and when service should start and end, we are having "church." God wants to convict the hearts of men and women to let them know that He loves them and that He is Lord.

I sat in church for years, wondering how a loving God could want someone like me, but the truth is He does. The Father left His throne in the person of Jesus Christ just to come to get you and me. The blood had to be purchased, and now that it has been, I no longer feel like I do not deserve His love.

Now Jesus Christ is sitting at the right hand of the throne, making intercession on our behalf (see Hebrews 7:25). I have learned how to tap into the Godhead through prayer, fasting, and His Word. The Holy Spirit is now on the scene to help us. He lives inside of every believer once we accept Jesus Christ as Lord and Savior.

The person of the Holy Spirit comes to lead and guide us into all truth (see John 16:13). This is a news flash: the body of Christ requires His help! We must allow room for Him to show up when we invite Him in. Once we give Him back His glory, we will see souls saved, lives transformed, miracles, signs, and wonders. Stop thinking and acting like I did as a churchgoer. God wants His glory back in the Body of Christ!

The Naked Truth
*****

Church people die and go to hell every day!

Michele's Heart
*****

Lord, I thank You that people matter to me. You said that he who wins souls is wise. Lord, You called me out of darkness, so if I have to snatch people or even make them feel uncomfortable to win them by any means necessary ... Lord, send me. Here I am!

Exposing the Lies
Favor ain't fair.

7. Why does the next person get what you have or more, after all you have been through?

> Saying, "These last men have worked only one hour, and you made them equal to us who have borne the burden and the heat of the day."
> —Matthew 20:12

CHAPTER 7

God's Favor

First, I want to say if it were not for God's favor on our lives, we would not be able to write this book. We thank God that we do not have disease in our bodies. We understand that grace is God's unmerited favor. We do not deserve it, but we sure are thankful for it. God's favor is not like a person's favor. A person's favor is conditional (as long as I do what they say, I remain in their good grace).

I love God and His Word. As I mentioned, Tim and I started a ministry in 2007 outside of the four walls of the church, and it is called Repairer of the Breach. The ministry is known for its prayer, praise, and worship unto God. God has called us to help rebuild and restore the homes of families (see Isaiah 58:12). We tell our testimony wherever we go because we want the world to know God can heal and deliver marriages and people if we allow Him.

At our meetings, lives are changed, and deliverance takes place. Tim and I always want more of God when we experience His power. Whether we are in someone's home, a clubhouse, or out in the parking lot, God always leaves us refreshed. When we give God time in our services, He always shows up and shows out. We have an assignment for ministry in and outside the walls of the church. We have several testimonies about God's favor during our times of ministry.

I ran for Satan and the things of the world when I was in the world. I am going to run for God even harder. We believe in giving back and making disciples out of people. We understand that the race is not given to the swift or the strong but he who endures to the end (see Ecclesiastes 9:11). We make time for what we want in life, and we have made a decision that we will serve the Lord (see Joshua 24:15). Wisdom from Bishop Derek Grier follows: "We complain about being in church for an hour and a half, but we give the man forty hours a week with no complaints."

God Opened the Doors to Our New Home

In 2002, Tim and I sought the Lord about purchasing a single-family home. God gave the green light, and we came into agreement to believe God by faith for the new home. We put a contract on the house and put $500 down. Once we were assigned a lot, we poured oil into the foundation and wrote our names in the dirt. We declared God's Word in Ezekiel 36 over our house. In this process, our faith was put to the test. In January 2003, we went to the closing to sign the paperwork. We were informed that we needed $30,000 for a down payment.

Homeless, we ran from pillow to post between friends, family, and hotel rooms. We had no money because we used the money from selling our townhome to pay off all our debt. A lower debt ratio would ensure that we qualified and would be approved for a new house. We went back to God and reminded Him that He told us to move. We told Him, "We are homeless now." We asked God what He wanted us to do. God said, "Have faith in Me."

When God speaks a thing, He will bring it to pass. Do you have the faith to believe when someone tells you no and all doors are shut? Our faith grew leaps and bounds. The mortgage company was in a bonded agreement with us since they let us sign all the documents. We believed God would turn our situation around. We stood on the promise that God had spoken. Also, we were mindful of the words that we spoke, realizing we would have whatever we said.

God did what He said He would do! We have been in the same home for more than sixteen years. To God be all the glory!

I Will Not Give Anyone God's Glory

We were approached about sharing our testimony with a professor, to be aired on a national television show. We were excited because we love sharing our testimony of how God saved our marriage. We believe in giving hope to others as we tell how the power of God led us into all truth concerning life and godliness. We received a call from the professor with one request before the taping. She requested that we allow her to interview us and then lie and say that several sessions with her restored our marriage.

I do not sugarcoat or water down anything, especially when it comes to God's glory. I am very careful about what the world calls white lies. Satan is the father of lies, and I do not want any part of being in his family. Just imagine if I had gone along with that lie. God would not be obligated to cover me. I would have been outside of His safety.

Giving God's glory to someone else could have led me to lying, cheating, stealing, robbing, killing, and sleeping with more men or women than I could write about. When we reject God, He allows us to become lovers of ourselves (see Romans 1). By not filling our hearts with God and His Word, we give the one demon that was cast out an opportunity to come back with seven (see Matthew 12:45).

Tim and I understand that our marriage was restored by God and Him alone. We are not willing to give credit to anyone but God. The Bible says in Matthew 16:26, "For what profit is it to a man if he gains the whole world, and loses his own soul?" You cannot put a value on God's glory because it cost Him everything. Some people wonder what is going on in their lives when trouble comes. Could it be that they have taken the credit for what God has done?

When God brings you out, do not forget to say, "Thank You!" Also, have confidence that it was His grace and mercy. In spite of ourselves, God has been so good to us. We should not choose to forget what God has done and how far He has brought us. I am very much aware that it was no one but God that delivered me from a life of sin and destruction.

Favor Is Fair in God's Eyes

Favor is fair in God's eyes. When you let go of things and people, then God can interrupt your life to really show you off. I had to learn that when God removes something, it is for my betterment. God is way smarter than we are. He tells us His ways are so much higher than ours, but if we are carnal minded, we try to bring Him to our level.

God told me I was going to be let go from my job that I loved. I had been working from home for the last six years at that time. God said to me, "Stop spending, start saving, and pay your bills off." One year later, I was let go from that job. I was not shocked because God will not have you caught off guard (see 2 Corinthians 2:11). The Holy Spirit is wise, and we should listen to Him.

I really started enjoying and trusting in the life I was living. God had a better plan for me. I thought this was good, but God had something better. I had to totally depend on God because my income went from $5,000 per month to $2,000 per month. I never lost a thing. I took a trip to Paris (first-class flight), and we had a family trip to Florida.

God can do more when we put things in His hands. My faith has increased because God kept His promises to me. God was showing me that He really is my Source. Within three days of being let go, I was working. Within six months, I had started my own billing company, Covenant Claim Center. Additionally, I signed a three-year contract during that same time frame. Favor is fair.

During this transition, I was looking for another source of income. I contacted a friend, who told me about a job opening. I called and spoke with a lady, but the available position was clinical. I had a wonderful conversation with the lady, and she promised to let me know if a position became available. Later on, she called me back and asked if I could meet with her to talk.

When I met with her, I did not realize that it was an interview. She and another young lady began to ask me questions. When she mentioned pay, I realized this was a position for me. The magic question was when she asked about my education level. They appeared shocked when they learned that I did not have a high school diploma or GED.

A few days later, I received a call saying that I was being hired. I was told that I could work on my education later, but in the meantime, they really wanted me for a specific position. A high school diploma or GED were both prerequisites for the job that I received. The fact they hired me was because of no one but God.

If I had not been released from my job, I would not have had time to write this book. I would not have started my own business. God has a plan and purpose for our life that is beautiful, if we let Him. I see God's hand all over my testimony, and I choose to brag about my Daddy, Abba Father.

"Ye are of God, little children, and have overcome them: because greater is he that is in you, than he that is in the world" (1 John 4:4 KJV).

I have left churches, jobs, and relationships, and I truly realize nothing just happens to happen.

The Power of Agreement

My husband was diagnosed with a pinched nerve in his neck and needed surgery. On the morning before, I went into prayer, and the Lord said, "Come into agreement with Tim about the surgery because the enemy is going to try to take Tim's life." I told Tim that same morning what the Lord had told me. I immediately called the doctor's office to get his appointment the next day. They called our insurance company and received the authorization that same day.

The surgery was scheduled for 8:00 a.m., and we arrived at 5:00 a.m. The procedure went well, but Tim experienced postsurgical complications. I was told that recovery time would take one hour. After about two hours, I told the nurse that I needed to get back there with Tim.

When I saw Tim, he was barely conscious. I began to pray and talk to him. I told him that I wanted him to wake up. His body started to respond to what I was telling him to do.

I went back to God and asked, "How is the enemy going to take Tim's life? He is not the giver of life?" He showed me in His Word about the power of agreement and the authority we have over each other's bodies as husband and wife (see Matthew 18:19–20; 1 Corinthians 7:4). Tim did recover from this setback; however, we did not know that we would experience a similar situation.

Here We Go Again

Following the first surgery, Tim was scheduled to have surgery again, but this time on his hand as a result of the pinched nerve in his neck. Prior to the surgery, I asked him if he had asked me if he could have surgery on his hand. I did not like the answer Tim gave me. The Lord told me to get in bed and go to sleep because he knew I was going to talk too much and cause an argument. I obeyed the Lord and went to sleep.

Our friend and brother Tracy Bell drove us to the hospital on the morning of the surgery. Upon our arrival, I told the nurse to ensure that the doctor did not begin the surgery before speaking with me. Once I was allowed to go into the surgical preparation area, I also requested that Tim not be given any type of anesthesia or pain blocker before talking with the doctor. The personnel assigned to begin Tim's anesthesia moved on to the next patient.

The surgeon came in to exam Tim's hand. He inquired about the movement he observed in his hand. He realized that four weeks ago, there was not any motion noticeable in that hand. I was silently praying, "Come on, Jesus!" The surgeon then said to Tim, because his hand had improved, surgery was not advised at that time. Tim got dressed, and we went home. To God be all the glory!

The Naked Truth
*****

God is your only Source to resources.

Michele's Heart
*****

Heavenly Father, I thank You that You give seed to the sower. I thank You that I have learned to trust You even when I cannot see You. You truly are my Source in life. Thank You that promotion does not come from the east or the west but from You. Thank You that You have established my ways, and now I put my trust in You. Thank You, Lord, that You own everything. Since I belong to You, I have access to all Your promises of health, wealth, and peace of mind. God, I put my life in Your hands, and I am a better person because of You. We win in You, and the enemy is defeated. Thank You for the strength to pull down strongholds. We have the victory in Jesus's name. Amen.

Exposing the Lies
Beauty never fades.

8. Because I am beautiful, I can …

Charm is deceitful and beauty is passing, but a woman
who fears the Lord, she shall be praised.
—Proverbs 31:30

CHAPTER 8

Deglamorizing Sin

D o not get stuck on what you look like. There are many beautiful women and handsome men in the world. How many times have we seen someone glamorous appear fabulous but so sad and depressed? We often hear about those stories on the television show *Unsung*. This show is about people who did great things but received little or no recognition for their work. Let us discuss how to make ourselves look awesome in our appearance, but in the end, it really does not matter.

Our beauty, if not tamed, is like a loaded 9 mm gun, which is deadly if it goes off. Let us disarm the weapon of vain beauty. First, we must make sure it is on safety mode at all times, unless it is going to be fired. Check to make sure there are no rounds in the chamber. Next, take it off the safety mode and hold the button down to open and slide the chamber back. Once the barrel has been removed, the pin can be taken out. In the same manner, let us take the poison out of vain beauty.

Hollywood makes sin look fun and glamorous. Again, I remind you that sin produces death. I believed the lie that I had to weigh 135 pounds. I also believed that I had to have long hair and perfectly manicured nails. I thought I had to be ready for the runway at all times. The billboards always appear flawless, but what you and I do not see are the touchups that are made to those photos.

God stripped my thinking and showed me that trying to keep up with Hollywood was actually weighing me down. He stripped my thinking that sin was fun and glamorous. There is nothing pretty about a foundation built on glamour. If your life is not built on the solid foundation of Jesus Christ, it will crack and peel. These are some of the thoughts that He stripped away:

S—seductive, sexuality, sin
T—trickery, temptation, torment
R—robbery, residue, reprobate, reproach, revolt
I—indignation, injustice, iniquity, idolatry
P—provoking, pride, perverse, perplexed

Glamour: magic, seeming mysterious, bewitched charm.
—*Webster's New World Dictionary*

I have heard Christians talk about things of the world, such as television shows, celebrities, making money, and so on. When I ask them about a scripture, they do not know as much about the Bible. When Christians glorify the things of the world, we are operating with a carnal mind.

All that is in the world glorifies the flesh. I went from playing with Barbie dolls to trying to live up to the Hollywood supermodel. I chose to stop competing with images on television and tap into who God called me to be: Michele T. Turner.

"Put on the whole armor of God, that you may be able to stand against the wiles of the devil" (Ephesians 6:11).

Truth

When I think about the armor and its truth as the Word of God for protection, I think of a woman putting on her makeup. We arm ourselves by putting on eyeshadow, lashes, eyeliner, foundation, concealer, and lipstick. Maybelline declares they are the truth because they promise thicker and longer lashes. It is waterproof, and Maybelline has also labeled their lashes "The Big Shot." I wear eyelashes in order to define my eyes because I have naturally short lashes.

Righteousness

Righteousness reminds me of applying eyeliner. Eyeliner is drawn on, and the eyes stand out. The eyeshadow also makes the eyes stand out and draws attention, providing a bold and peaceful look. You can play with one or multiple colors to give your face that look. In a crowd you will stand out when you have on a bold or bright color.

Too many times, I operated in my own righteousness, better known as self-righteousness. I only wanted to glorify myself. I have learned today that my righteousness has nothing to do with me. I thought I was right, but in fact I was wrong. Righteousness is defined as right standing with God (see Romans 3:22).

I was waiting on Hollywood to approve my righteousness, but my righteousness only comes through the person of Jesus Christ. When we think that we are glamorous in our self-righteousness, the book of Isaiah tells us that it is as filthy rags (see Isaiah 64:6).

Faith

On our lips we have the option to use matte line lipstick because it lasts longer. Just like the test of time, do you have long-lasting faith? For years, I thought faith was something you could see. I felt because I did not kill anyone and was a good person, faith would work for me. I never thought about how I lived but thought faith should work for me as long as I called on the name of the Lord. In reality, the just shall live by faith (see Hebrews 10:38).

My youngest daughter is named Faith. I named her that because

I knew it would take the power of God to get me through having a baby after sixteen years since my last child was born. I always said if God decided to rewrite the Bible, I want to be in the book of Hebrews because of my Faith.

The fundamental fact of existence is that this trust in God, this faith, is the firm foundation under everything that makes life worth living. It's our handle on what we can't see. The act of faith is what distinguished our ancestors, set them above the crowd (Hebrews 11:1–2, The Message Bible).

Salvation

We have our salvation, which is the foundation on which we build our Christian lives. The world offers different types of foundations, including liquid, powder, or spray. Once you put your foundation on, it covers up most of your blemishes. Other religions say there are many gods, but we serve the true and living God.

"But the Lord is the true God; he is the living God, the eternal King. When he is angry, the earth trembles; the nations cannot endure his wrath" (Jeremiah 10:10 NIV).

Word of God

We are nothing without our concealer, which is the Word of God. Just like concealer, it holds everything in place. So even if people rub up against you, it will not smear or get on their clothes. The Word of God, Jesus Christ, handled everything by dying for our sins. The Word of God is my lifeline; I use it all the time. It is not just a good story but God manifested in the flesh.

All Made Up

Now that we have this made-up face, what do you see in the mirror? What is looking back at you? Do you identify with this person?

Occasionally, I have had my face "beat" professionally by friends when attending special events. They would explain what they were putting on my face and why. Once they were finished, they would pass me a mirror and ask me how I liked the look. I do not really wear a lot of makeup, so I had to get used to the look. If they applied too much, I would ask them to take some of it off.

On Saturdays, I would sleep pretty and wear the makeup to church on Sunday. I wanted that same look because that was how fantasy Barbie looked when she awoke. That was my problem; it was all about the glam look. As a woman, I knew what to put on and what to take off. Now as a woman of God, He has taught me how not to cover up my blemishes. He has taught me that beauty is more on the inside than the outside.

"She is clothed with strength and dignity, and she laughs without fear of the future" (Proverbs 31:25 NLT).

This is how God clothes us! There is no designer like the Lord! I am a fashion model for the Lord, and I wear my garment wherever I go. I am light and refuse to be darkness. There is no money or bribe that can cause me to turn my garment of praise in for the spirit of heaviness (see Isaiah 61:3).

We can walk the red carpet and the runway for Jesus. You do not have to be involved in a scandal or build an empire to show the world that you are glamorous! I am fearfully and wonderfully made (see Psalm 139). We are in the world, but I refuse to be of it any longer.

Deglamorizing Process

I would advise you to go look in the mirror again. Do you like what you see?

Remove the eyeshadow, lashes, lipstick, and the rest of your makeup. The only way the enemy will no longer rob you is by putting on the full armor of God. You have to allow Jesus to wash the sin off of you. It is your choice. You can either go back home and lie down with the same garbage of sin, or you can wash yourself today with the Word of God and be set free. Allowing God to give you a glow and an anointing that makeup cannot do.

"The Lord make His face shine upon you, and be gracious to you; The Lord lift up His countenance upon you, And give you peace" (Numbers 6:25-26).

This is what we really want to make us glamorous.

Removing the Makeup

After cleaning your face of the natural makeup, sometimes your skin tingles because of the cleanser you chose to use to detox. God needs to detox you. It is up to you whether you take the detox or not. A detox for me is like a time of fasting. During a fast, for a period of time I abstain from and get rid of toxic or unhealthy substances.

After the Detox

God wants to restructure the foundation. Today, women have all types of surgeries, including liposuction to the lips, building up cheekbones, and even permanent eyebrows. God wants to give us a sure foundation so that we are able to stand against the wiles of the devil.

We are not putting on this armor to wear it just to look good. When the trials of life—adultery, fornication, jealousy, and unforgiveness—come against us, we will know how to build a sure foundation. You will know how to apply the Word of God. We will be delivered in the areas that will also help others. I believe that it is important to help someone else after you get your foundation built. The idea is once I am strong, I will have something to offer the next woman.

"Let your speech always be with grace, seasoned with salt, that you may know how you ought to answer each one" (Colossians 4:6).

I may not be assigned to everyone, but I am assigned to someone. I must stay focused on my assignment so that the person I am assigned to will not have lazy eyes or falling cheekbones that will need Botox. The Word of God will strengthen your face, not to make it hard but so that it is soft. People will be able to glean from the beauty. The glory of God will allow your face to transform, and at every facet, someone will be able to pull fruit off of your tree.

Trust and see now that your foundation is solid. They will not vomit after talking to you. They will not feel that you are judgmental, but coming to you will build them up. The world has torn them down, and they are malnourished.

I can now say like the Apostle Paul in Romans 8:37, "I am more than a conqueror." I want to win for my sister! I will get in the trenches with my sister so that we can win together. I want my marriage to be strong. I do not want to be fake. I do not want my marriage to be like that makeup that you sleep in all night long. I want my marriage to be a solid foundation that other marriages can glean from. I want to be the Ruth to my Boaz. I want to be the woman of God that God has called me to be in my church and with my children.

This foundation that God will build is not plastic. It will not crack. It will stand the test of time no matter what I go through. My face will not harden, and my lips will be soft so that I know how to answer and give an account. I know how to be accountable.

I love myself today because I have denied myself, picked up my cross, and am following Jesus. I have made a choice to strip off the world's ways. I am throwing those ways off of me. I have put on the armor. God has given me His Word that I may be a testimony to the world to see what a new creature in Christ looks like, if we allow Him to redeem us.

Your story is not my story, but we all have a story to tell about the goodness of Jesus and all that He has done for us. Your glory looks good on you!

The Naked Truth
*****

When you know your value, never let anyone devalue you. Jesus paid it all, and it cost Him everything. Know your worth!

Michele's Heart
*****

Father, I thank You that You created us in your image and after Your likeness. Therefore, we are beautiful people. Thank You for clothes, makeup, and things that we adorn ourselves with. May we never desire outer beauty more than inner peace and joy. I thank You that You have clothed us with Your love. I am beautiful in You, and You are my strength and shield.

Exposing the Lies
It is a generational curse.

9. Your children will be just like you. They will make the same mistakes and live under a generational curse.

Behold, children are a heritage from the Lord,
the fruit of the womb is a reward.
—Psalm 127:3

CHAPTER 9

The Fruit of My Womb

It truly is a lie that your children will be just like you. They may look like you, but what you put inside of them and push them toward makes the difference. I did not push out these three beautiful babies to become failures. I have birthed three gifted and talented human beings.

I always remind my children that they are from my cloth. I tell them that they have been cut different in order to do different things. I teach them to never settle for any less than the best in life.

The curse has been broken over their lives. The older two did not have children as teenagers. They have both graduated from high school, and obtained degrees in higher education. They still have conversations with me for godly wisdom.

I was not a good example for my two older children as they grew up. I purposely worked to change my life to show them a better example. I have not tried to prove to them that I am perfect. I do not need them to validate any of my decisions, whether good or bad. I am grateful that I learned to train them up in the way they should go (see Proverbs 22:6).

Many parents feel guilty, and their children control them. I have talked with my children, sharing with them before I ever shared with the world. They too have made mistakes, but we are living life one day at a time and on purpose.

My Testimony

"Her children rise up and call her blessed; Her husband also, and he praises her" (Proverbs 31:28).

All three of my children know about my testimony, and they love me even the more. They understand that this book will help change lives. They were each born with a purpose. God reminded me that each one of my children had an amazing story behind their delivery. My first baby was premature. With the second baby, my cervix would not dilate. And with the third baby, my water broke, but twelve hours later, we were praying against her getting jaundice.

Children are a blessing from the Lord. "A woman, when she is in labor, has sorrow because her hour has come; but as soon as she has given birth to the child, she no longer remembers the anguish, for joy that a human being has been born into the world." (John 16:21)

I am truly blessed to be able to share with the world about my blessed children! Prior to having my daughter Quanika, I had several abortions during my teenage years. Finally, my dad told me not to have another abortion, and I listened. My firstborn child arrived when I was sixteen years old. I was a child having a child.

This was a changing point in my life because I knew this child was special. I had to give her the best life that I possibly could. Quanika Michele was born prematurely during the second trimester of my pregnancy on June 18, 1985. She weighed only three pounds. She immediately dropped to a pound. In comparison, think about a pound of butter. That was the size of my baby.

In that same year, the *Washington Post* was reporting on young mothers having premature babies. The article included my story as a teenage mother:

<1985 – The Washington Post Newspaper Article>
A nurse holding Quanika

I stayed with Quanika in the hospital for two months. She was hooked up to numerous monitors. The doctors were especially concerned about her heart. Upon her release from the hospital, she was still connected to the heart monitor. Every turn she made caused the monitor to alarm. This alarm automatically alerted the hospital, and an ambulance was sent to my home.

My family said to me, "There is nothing wrong with this baby!" We removed the monitor from her tiny body. She survived as a result of the mixture of her will to live (she is a fighter) and my love for this once miniscule human being (that I could hold in one hand). Quanika is thirty-four years old and has never had any problems with her heart.

Education

I dropped out of school to raise Quanika. My mom moved so many times I skipped school for a whole year. My parents did not realize I was not going to school. I tried night school and dropped out of that program.

In 1986, I decided to do something different. I was determined to fight for myself and Quanika to have a better life. Things started to change for me because I started viewing life with a purpose. I attended Strayer College, taking classes to become a clerk typist. I am proud to say that in 1987, I was awarded a certificate as a clerk typist.

I was a teenager raising a precious gift from God. I was determined not to become a "welfare chick." I had no desire to raise my baby off the public system, even if this meant doing so alone. Quanika and I always did well because of my diligence and hard work.

I never asked for child support. I pushed past my mistakes and did what I needed to do to raise Quanika without the help of the system or a baby daddy.

Today, Quanika has a master's degree in business and is pursuing her DBA. She is the business owner of Nina's Boutique. She is determined to not let life get the best of her. As I have already stated, she is a fighter. History did not repeat itself with her. She is successful, beautiful, powerful, and a smart young lady. I will say so myself!

Tim took my daughter Quanika and loved her as if she was his own. Any man can make a baby, but it takes a real man to father a child. We have never acknowledged Tim as her stepfather because he was not trying to replace her biological dad. He was just being himself as he stepped up to the plate, marrying me and making her his own. Tim has been in our daughter's life since she was six months old.

I love seeing this woman of God doing ministry. She leads the children's dance ministry at Grace Church, Virginia. She also has the gift of discernment. She is a selfless giver, giving away a $1,500 scholarship each year for Project Prom. She also donates to a local homeless shelter every year. She enjoys giving back to others.

My One and Only Son

Timothy Wayne Turner Jr. is my son, and there is so much to say about him. Tim Jr. is the one "whom I love" (John 13:23). When I was out doing me, I could remember my mom telling me that he said,

"All I want for Christmas is for my mom to come home." During that time, I was living with a young man, and Quanika and Tim Jr. lived with Tim Sr.

When Tim Jr. was little, he would say he wanted to become a preacher. His childhood dream was to play professional basketball, whether NBA, overseas teams, or ABA. The team did not matter; he just loved the game. God has allowed us to see His hand of mercy. Tim Jr. was drafted to play for the Baltimore Spartans in July 2018. He currently plays for the Fredericksburg Grizzlies. Tim Jr. has coached at Grace Preparatory Private School and Brooke Point High School. He has a bachelor's degree in business administration. He is doing very well for himself and enjoying life.

There are a number of things I want to say about this young man. The main thing is he loves his mother! I am including a song that he wrote to me:

"My First Love"
By Timothy Turner Jr.

My first love,
well because you loved me first,
Celebrated my best and accepted my worst.

My first love,
well you gave me life, right?
Love at first sight,
in my darkest hour you were my nightlight.

My first love, I watched you elevate;
from Chuck Brown and Erykah Badu to staying up late,
head in this Book and a prayer closet for your families' sake.
Doing whatever it took to make you great.

My first love, I swear they are not built like you,
I'm not talking the hair styles and rocking 'fits like you.

I'm talking about ya' smile and how you effect a room and
I'm talking about all ya' truths and how respect comes too.

My first love, I ain't been the best of the three
but as your only son you instilled the best in me;
like how to treat a lady and don't be making no babies,
stop all that cussing on the court and watch that boy
'cause he shady.
To chase your dreams Babyboy,
it's gone come, don't stress;
we are standing on a mountain of no's for one yes.

My first love, to be honest,
I really ain't wanna share you
'cause this world so cold
I ain't wanna hear them compare you.
But who am I to spare you?
When God said,
"He'd never give you anything to over bear you,
So, I dared you.

My first love,
you taught me to see opportunity
in closed doors
and this ain't a game
but I got two sisters to play for.
So, family mean for all mine,
I'll lay yours!

My first love, you've been everything
and more than I could ask of a mother,
This is my dear Mama
and there will never be another.

Babyboy

Faith Michele Is Born

Who would have thought that I would have a baby after all these years? "'For I know the plans I have for you,' declares the Lord, 'plans to prosper you and not to harm you, plans to give you hope and a future'" (Jeremiah 29:11). Well, God said He knew me when I was in my mother's womb (Psalm 139:13). God also knew that He would bless Tim and me with Faith Michele Turner.

When I first got pregnant with Faith, I was somewhat angry with God. I could not imagine starting over with a baby. I do not have a good tolerance with babies. Now I cannot imagine life without her. Faith is such a joy!

During my pregnancy, doctors told me that I had high cholesterol, high blood pressure, and diabetes. God allowed me to overcome the report of the doctors. I did not have to take medication. I controlled these conditions with diet and exercise.

Faith was born with about twenty-five guests in the delivery room. There was a spiritual battle going on. I went into labor at 6:00 p.m. on August 24, 2004, but Faith was not delivered until August 25, 2004, at 7:11 a.m. I had been in labor for more than eight hours when I was given the epidural. The doctor began to worry that she would have jaundice because my water had broken ten hours earlier.

Finally, the doctor on call said she was going to give me a C-section delivery. Immediately I began to cry. I told my husband to not allow them to cut me. Once my ob-gyn doctor arrived at six in the morning, Faith Michele was born in one hour and eleven minutes.

Fifteen years later, and this young lady loves God. I love our time that we share together with the Lord. I love when we minister together. It is priceless to see the God in her.

The Naked Truth
*****

Children are like a sponge; what you put in
them is what you will get out of them.

Michele's Heart
*****

Father, I thank You that You have given me a second and third
chance to get it right with my children. Thank You that You called
me to be Quanika, Tim Jr., and Faith's mom. I desire to help nurture
and cultivate decisions to make them better people in the world
today. Always allow them to see good in others as You pull out the
best in them. They are not average; they are world changers. In
Jesus's name.

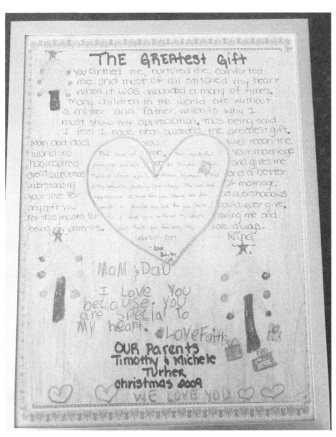

A collage of words from the children

Exposing the Lies
You cannot overcome infidelity.

10. It is over!

Can two walk together, unless they are agreed?
—Amos 3:3

CHAPTER 10

We Believe

Y ou may want to debate us. However, we have taken our case to the Supreme Court, and the Judge is Jesus Christ. God hates divorce, and Tim and I feel the same. The Judge has said, "Order in the courtroom." He has made His decision based on the facts. Docket 1: Jesus Christ died for our marriage. Docket 2: We have now denied ourselves, picking up our crosses, and are following Him all the way. Docket 3: The verdict is not guilty.

This is our preamble:

We the Turners of the United States of America, in order to form a perfect marriage, and establish forgiveness, remove insecurities, instill honesty and integrity. Providing for the common good of marriage, promoting love and, securing blessings of liberty to ourselves and others. We do ordain and establish this marriage before the people of God.

We believe God has allowed us to write this book with the help of the Holy Spirit to be a blessing to the world. No one would believe the things we have gone through, so we thought we would start out with Michele's life but our testimony. In November 2019, we celebrated thirty-two years of marriage. Michele's story is my story.

Tim

No one in their right mind would believe the two of us would still be together after all we have been through. None of our friends thought we would stay together. I never thought we would stay together. In one of our most difficult seasons, I was stationed eight hundred miles from home. I did not know what I was going to do being so far away from my family. I always said that God had better things for me.

I would go to church and cry out to God, and God would say, "You have to forgive her," and I would say, "But, Lord, I cannot." He would say, "Yes you can." I said, "I cannot forget what has happened." God said, "I said forgive, not forget. So, I forgave and began to pray that God would keep her safe; she is the mother of my children. I have always loved Michele unconditionally and wanted nothing but the best for her and us.

Things were not going as planned, but I never wanted anything to happen to Michele while she was out there in the streets. We had been going through it for years, and I was tired and lonely, but I still had hope for my marriage. Finally, one day I felt like I did not want to be married anymore. I went to see a lawyer, but God was in that because she only wanted money that I did not have. I did not follow through with the lawyer.

God told me to forgive her, yet I still felt like my marriage was over. I began to get sick and lost weight. I could not believe we were here again. This time it looked like the point of no return. She was living with another man. The Bible says hope deferred makes the heart sick (see Proverbs 13:12).

I was not trying anymore for the marriage, but I continued to go to church for myself. My heart was not as hard anymore. I thought I could be her friend if that was what God had planned for us. I always felt God was going to bring her back. I just did not know when.

One day she told me that she was leaving because she felt as though I deserved better. She said she loved me but was not in love with me anymore. I said, "Go, but you will be back!"

I knew I had been nothing but good to her and no other man would love her the way I loved her. When she called me one year later and said she wanted to come back home, it was easy to say yes. God had given me the peace I needed to say yes. I did not know what would happen, but I had to trust God and put it in His hands. I said, "Lord, I cannot run this race by myself!" We had to both be willing to run this race together. I did not think about how it made me look or what anyone said about me. I remembered what I said in my vows when we got married. This is what kept me.

I believed that God can do anything but fail. Because He saved our marriage; I know He can save any marriage. You have to believe that He will. I made my vows unto God, so the test of what I said on November 14, 1987, was time for me to put up or shut up. My dad left me, and I vowed I would never leave my family, even while she was out there running the streets. I took care of my kids because I did not want another man raising my children. I knew my kids were already hurting, but they were young, so I did not discuss this with them.

Since that day Michele came back through those doors, we have been trusting and believing God every step of the way. We have had some bumps and bruises, but Lord knows I have not seen that person that I was willing to just be friends with.

Our Declaration

We believe that we are better together. We wanted to show the world what God can do with two people who are willing to submit their lives unto Him. We believe that we can get through any problem the world throws at us. We believe that we were meant to be together. We believe that it is the truth that sets you free. We believe that we are more than conquerors through Christ, who truly has strengthened us. We believe that our children deserved better.

We believe that God said let the two become one, and nothing should or would be able to separate us. Life is a teacher, and it sure has taught us some principles concerning marriage, love, forgiveness, longsuffering, and self-control. We believe our marriage is just like this book—raw. We know it will help transform the world and everything God intended for our marriage to become.

We believe that not everyone could have gone through what we went through. We believe if you put Christ in your marriage, nothing is impossible. We believe our marriage is just like our wedding rings because everything has come back full circle.

We believe we are fulfilling our purpose here on earth. We truly are better together, with you in mind. We believe our marriage will be a blessing to some and an eye-opener for others. Most of all, we hope that you see Jesus, the great I Am, in all of it. We believe that God has given us the faith to move mountains.

We believe that it is not over until God says it is over. We believe we can have whatever we say. We believe in the power of love. Neither Tim nor I deserve love, but we now understand that love covers and will keep us if we want to be kept. We define love as follows:

L—letting go of the past
O—overcoming and beating all odds
V—victory is ours
E—exercising our right to love one another

The Naked Truth
*****

I believe the world does not have enough people believing in the power of us (marriage). Everyone is in it for me, myself, and I. I believe we are a force to be reckoned with and definitely better.

Michele's Heart
*****

Father, I thank You that You are a God of second chances. Daddy, thank You for believing and encouraging us to keep going strong, no matter what the world said. We believe that all things are possible. We love You forever.

Momma,

On June 19, 2019, you went to sleep and did not wake up, just as you told me you would leave this earth. J. T., girl, you know that I will always love you. You have always been by my side through the good and bad. I will love you forever and ever.

You left this world better than it was. You truly were a woman of God. The faith you stood on in your darkest moments in life is undeniable.

You told me and everyone for the last five years that you were coming off of dialysis … and you did. I cannot say you left too soon; you left when you got ready. You told death and the doctors, "I am leaving on my own terms. Dialysis does not have the last say so!" You lived one month and three days after terminating dialysis. When you said you were quitting dialysis, you never looked back.

Momma girl, I want to be just like you when I grow up! I am truly grateful that we were able to do ministry together.

I will miss our Bible studies and prayer time together, but I will see you again for sure. You were dealt a hand, and you played your cards right. You won!

"O death, where is thy sting? O grave, where is thy victory?" (1 Corinthians 15:55, KJV).

We have the victory in Jesus Christ. I will see you again. I love you.

Your baby girl,

Michele

> But I do not want you to be ignorant, brethren, concerning those who have fallen asleep, lest you sorrow as others who have no hope. For if we believe that Jesus died and rose again, even so God will bring with Him those who sleep in Jesus.
> (1 Thessalonians 4:13–14)

A Note from My Friend Felissah Redfern, Who Knew Me When:

Thirty-five years ago, I met my best friend, Michele. From day one you have always taken care of me. At the time, I had to remind you that you were not my mother and we would both get a chuckle out of that.

You stood up for me and lied down beside me. Your consistent love and nurturing spirit came naturally. However, when you told me you were pregnant at such a young age, I became concerned. Not because I thought you would not be a great mother. My fear was because you were only a baby yourself.

Although, it appeared hard you unfailingly stayed in the fight. God blessed you with the understanding that no matter what the circumstances, never allow the situation to define who you are. God prepared you at a very young age to be that person who would love and care for His people and that is your purpose. I am very proud of you.

Felissah Redfern

NOTES

1   www.chemistryexplained.com
2   www.plymouthhospitals.nhs.uk.
3   www.latimes.com.
4   https://www.quora.com.
5   https://learning-center.homesciencetools.com.
6   www.aae.org.
7   www.naturalhealers.com.
8   https://www.goodhousekeeping.com/life/g2350/barbie-dolls-history-facts/.
9   www.itestcash.com.